Lotus Notes® 6

10
MINUTE
GUIDE

800 East 96th Street
Indianapolis, IN 46240

Jane Calabria, CLP and
Dorothy Burke, CLI

10 Minute Guide to Lotus Notes® 6

Copyright © 2003 by Que Publishing

International Standard Book Number: 0-7897-2675-0

Library of Congress Catalog Card Number: 2002111092

Printed in the United States of America

First Printing: January 2003

06   05   04   6   5   4   3

Trademarks

Warning and Disclaimer

Executive Editor
Candy Hall

Acquisitions Editor
Loretta Yates

Development Editor
Melanie Palaisa

Managing Editor
Charlotte Clapp

Project Editor
Tricia Liebig

Production Editor
Benjamin Berg

Proofreader
Carla Lewis

Technical Editor
John Palmer

Team Coordinator
Cindy Teeters

Interior Designer
Gary Adair

Cover Designer
Alan Clements

Page Layout
Joe Millay

Graphics
Tammy Graham

Contents

ABOUT THE AUTHORS

Jane Calabria has authored Lotus Notes books with Dorothy Burke and Rob Kirkland for many years. She was the series editor for the Macmillan Computer Publishing series of Lotus Notes and Domino R5 books. She is a CLP Notes Principal Application Developer with a principal certification as an application developer. She is also a Certified Microsoft User Specialist at the Expert level in Word and Excel. She and her husband, Rob Kirkland, own Stillwater Enterprises, Inc., a consulting firm located near Philadelphia, Pennsylvania. Jane and Rob are preeminent authors, speakers, and trainers on the topic of Lotus Notes and Domino and they conduct national training sessions and seminars. Jane is also the publisher and author (writing as Jane Kirkland) of Take A Walk® Books, a series of interactive, nature adventure books for kids. Learn more about her "other life" at www.takeawalk.com.

Dorothy Burke is a Certified Lotus Notes Instructor (CLI) and a CLP Notes Principal Application Developer with a principal certification as an application developer. She teaches Domino application development and has been an independent consultant and trainer since 1988. Dorothy is the editor for Jane's Take A Walk® children's books.

Together, Jane and Dorothy have co-authored more than 18 books including Que's *Certified Microsoft Office User Exam Guide*(s) for Microsoft Word 97, Microsoft Excel 97, and Microsoft Power Point 97. Also, *Microsoft Works 6-in-1*, *Microsoft Windows 95 6 in 1*, *Microsoft Windows 98 6-in-1*, *Using Microsoft Word 97*, and *Using Microsoft Word 2000*. Their Lotus Notes and Domino titles include Que's *Ten Minute Guide to Lotus Notes 4.6*, the *Ten Minute Guide to Lotus Notes Mail 4.6*, *Lotus Notes and the Internet 6 in 1*, *Sams Teach Yourself Lotus Notes*, *Teach Yourself Lotus Notes 5 in 10 Minutes*, *How to Use Lotus Notes R5*, *Teach Yourself Lotus Notes R5 in 24 Hours*, and *Teach Yourself Lotus Notes and Domino R5 Development in 21 Days*.

John Palmer (Technical Editor) is a Certified Lotus Professional, certified as an Application Developer (Principal Level—R5 & R4) and as a System Administrator (R5 & Principal level—R4). He owns John Palmer Associates in southeast Pennsylvania, providing Lotus Domino consulting services to medium and large size companies in the Delaware Valley. An author and technical editor, John also is a speaker at Lotus Notes conferences. His expertise is in integrating Domino and Web technologies, and developing complex Domino applications. John Palmer Associates is a Lotus Business Partner and can be found on the World Wide Web at www.jpassoc.net.

Melanie Palaisa (Development Editor) has been a technical writer and development editor for more than 15 years. She has been the development editor for several Que and Sams' series including Sams' and Que's Ten Minute Guides, Complete Idiot's Guides, 6 in 1, Easy, Special Edition Using, and Sams Teach Yourself.

She has joined Jane and Dorothy as the development editor for several books including *Microsoft Works 6-in-1*, *Microsoft Office 97 6 in 1*, *Using Microsoft Word 2000*, Que's *Ten Minute Guide to Lotus Notes 4.6*, the *Ten Minute Guide to Lotus Notes Mail 4.6*, and *Sams Teach Yourself Lotus Notes 5 in 24 Hours*. Melanie is also the development editor for Jane's Take A Walk® childrens' books.

Dedication

In memory of Jim Adair, who taught so very many the skills and joys of Lotus Notes. We will miss you and remember you always.

Acknowledgments

Our publisher remains a leader in Lotus Notes and Domino books and their commitment to provide quality books in a timely fashion to the Notes/Domino community has made working with their dedicated staff exciting. We thank them for the opportunities they provide us and the information they make available to Lotus Notes and Domino users at all levels of expertise.

WE WANT TO HEAR FROM YOU

As the reader of this book, *you* are our most important critic and commentator. We value your opinion and want to know what we're doing right, what we could do better, what areas you'd like to see us publish in, and any other words of wisdom you're willing to pass our way.

As an executive editor for Que, I welcome your comments. You can email or write me directly to let me know what you did or didn't like about this book—as well as what we can do to make our books better.

Please note that I cannot help you with technical problems related to the *topic* of this book. We do have a User Services group, however, where I will forward specific technical questions related to the book.

When you write, please be sure to include this book's title and author as well as your name, email address, and phone number. I will carefully review your comments and share them with the author and editors who worked on the book.

Email: feedback@quepublishing.com

Mail: Candy Hall
               Que Publishing
               800 East 96th Street
               Indianapolis, IN 46240 USA

For more information about this book or another Que title, visit our Web site at www.quepublishing.com. Type the ISBN (excluding hyphens) or the title of a book in the Search field to find the page you're looking for.

Introduction

WELCOME TO *10 MINUTE GUIDE TO LOTUS NOTES 6*

This book focuses on the basics of Lotus Notes and Domino; introduces general groupware, Notes, and email concepts; and shows you some advanced features of the program. You can work through the book lesson by lesson, building on your skills, or you can use the book as a quick reference when you want to perform a new task. Features and concepts are presented in tasks that take 10 minutes or less to complete.

If you are new to Notes, start at the beginning of the book. If you've used Notes before, you might want to skip the first few lessons and work from there. Use the Table of Contents and select the lessons that cover features of the program you haven't yet used. If you travel with Lotus Notes on your laptop, the compact size of this book is perfect for fitting into your laptop or notebook case.

WHO SHOULD USE THIS BOOK

10 Minute Guide to Lotus Notes 6 is for anyone who

- Has Lotus Notes 6 installed on their PC or laptop
- Needs to learn Notes 6 quickly
- Wants to explore some of the new features of Lotus Notes 6
- Needs a task-based Lotus Notes 6 tutorial
- Requires a compact Notes 6 reference guide

Conventions Used in This Book

In telling you to choose menu commands, this book uses the format *menu title*, *menu command*. For example, the statement "choose **File, Properties**" means "open the File menu and select the Properties command."

In addition, *10 Minute Guide to Lotus Notes 6* uses the following icons to identify helpful information:

PLAIN ENGLISH

New or unfamiliar terms are defined in "plain English."

TIMESAVER TIP

Look here for ideas that cut corners and confusion.

CAUTION

This icon identifies areas where new users often run into trouble and offers practical solutions to those problems.

From Here...

For more information on Lotus Notes, try these other books:

- *How to Use Lotus Notes 6*—A full-color visual tutorial for beginning Lotus Notes users.

- *Special Edition Using Lotus Notes and Domino 6*—The ultimate Lotus Notes companion for the advanced user, help desk personnel, consultant, administrator, and developer.

- *Lotus Notes and Domino R6 Development Unleashed*—The long-awaited high-end reference and learning guide to the advanced features of Domino development.

To learn about all of the Lotus Notes books, visit our Web site at
www.quepublishing.com.

For Lotus Notes press releases, technical information, and new product information, visit the Lotus Web sites. The following Lotus sites contain information relevant to the Notes client:

- www.Lotus.com—The Lotus home page, where you can find information on all Lotus products and services, including support and access to other Lotus Notes sites.

- www.lotus.com/education—The Lotus Education site, where you can find course descriptions, schedules, locations, certification information, and Lotus Authorized Education Centers for Lotus Notes and other Lotus Products.

- www.lotus.com/products/rnext.nsf—To learn about Notes features, download a trial, or check out some of the new features.

Lesson 1
Getting Started with Notes

In this lesson, you learn about Lotus Notes concepts, how to move around in Notes, and how to change and lock your password.

UNDERSTANDING THE NOTES CLIENT

Lotus Notes is based on client/server technology, which enables you to access, share, and manage information over a network. The network can consist of five or ten computers in your office building, cabled together, or it can consist of 30,000 computers across the United States, connected to one another in various ways. The software you're running on your PC is called the Lotus Notes 6 Client. It requests and receives information from the server, called the "Domino" server.

While working in Lotus Notes, all information, including your email, is stored in Domino applications, or databases. Notes *applications* are a collection of one or more *databases* that are designed to perform a specific function or work process (workflow). It is not unusual for people to use the terms *application* and *database* interchangeably. Your mail database, stored on the Domino server, is secure and only you have access to that database unless you change settings and allow others to have access. Other databases, such as the Help database, are accessible to many people, and many people can access such databases simultaneously.

The connection you have to the Domino server is similar to the connection you might have to your file server at work. Often, you store work that you have created in other software programs (such as

Microsoft Word) on the file server on your network at the office. For
example, you might save your Word documents on your F: drive,
which is actually space that is dedicated to you for storing files on the
file server.

Lotus Notes applications typically support or automate business functions by helping you create, collect, share, and manage almost any
kind of information. Notes applications can incorporate information
from external sources (such as Lotus spreadsheets), export data to
external databases (such as Approach), or contain documents (such as
Word).

This book assumes that you're working in your office, connected to a
Domino server; however, most of the procedures and tasks in this
book are similar, whether you're in your office or working from home.
If you're not attached to your network when you start Notes, the
Choose Location dialog box might appear. Choose **Home** as your
location and continue to work through this lesson, or go to Lesson 19,
"Using Notes Remotely," and see the section "Creating Location
Documents." Windows XP users may find an icon for "Lotus Notes"
at the top of their startup menu. This is a special icon that starts the
user's default email application. Clicking this icon will start Notes and
navigate directly to the email Inbox.

When you start Notes for the very first time, you might see the Lotus
Notes setup screen, in which case you should select option that says
"No thanks, just give me the defaults" so that you see the default
Welcome page as shown in Figure 1.1.

Through hotspots and bookmark buttons, the Welcome page provides
access to mail, calendars, Address Books, and To Do lists. The
Welcome page is customizable and you can add your favorite Web
sites or newsgroups. From here, you can also search databases or Web
sites, take a tour of Notes, and see what's new in Lotus Notes 6
Client. Table 1.1 describes the elements of the Notes window.

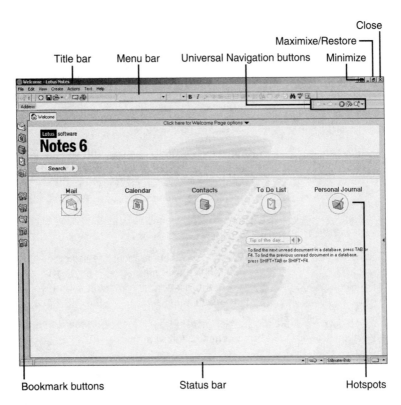

Close

Maximixe/Restore

Minimize

Title bar   Menu bar   Universal Navigation buttons

Bookmark buttons   Status bar   Hotspots

FIGURE 1.1

The Lotus Notes Welcome Page is your starting point to access mail, calendar, and all features of Notes.

TABLE 1.1   Notes Window Elements

Element	Function
Maximize button	Enlarges the Notes window to cover the Windows desktop; when the window is maximized, the Maximize button changes to a Restore button that you can click to return the window to its previous size.

TABLE 1.1   (continued)

Element	Function
Minimize button	Reduces the Notes window to a button on the Windows taskbar; to restore the window to its original size, click the button on the taskbar.
Close (X) button	Closes (exits) the Notes program.
Title bar	Contains program's name, and if you are in a database, describes where you are in that database; also displays a description of selected menu commands.
Menu	Contains the menus of commands you use to perform tasks in Notes.
Status bar	Presents information about the selected item, shows error messages (if any), displays your location, and indicates when you have new mail.
Hotspots	Text or picture that you click on to perform an action or follow a link.
Bookmark Buttons	Each button opens bookmark page or a list of bookmarks to access documents, sites, or databases.
Bookmark	Opens a database or task when you click the bookmark.
Universal Navigation	Provide the means to navigate buttons through Notes, going forward or backward, stopping an activity, refreshing pages, searching, or opening URLs.

NAVIGATING IN NOTES

There are several tools for moving around and opening tasks and databases in Notes. They include hotspots, as you will find on the Basics page of the Welcome screen, navigation buttons, and bookmarks.

The hotspots on the Welcome page are pretty self-explanatory: Click on the Mail hotspot to open your mail database, or click on the Calendar hotspot to view your calendar.

Navigation buttons are located in the upper-right corner of the Notes window. When you point at one of the buttons, a tip appears to tell you the name of the button and the keyboard shortcut that performs the same function. Table 1.2 provides a short explanation of each button.

TABLE 1.2   The Navigation Buttons

Click Here	Name	Description
	Go Back	Returns to the previous page, document, or task. Right-click to see a drop-down menu of places you can go back to; select one to go there.
	Go Forward	Takes you to the task, page, or document that was displayed prior to your clicking Go Back. Right-click to see a drop-down menu of the places you can go forward to; select one to go there.
	Stop	Interrupts the current program activity.
	Refresh	Refreshes the current document, page, or view with the latest data.
	Search	Displays a drop-down menu of search choices to find what you need. You can search the current view, document, or page; your Notes domain; or the Web.

Bookmark buttons are located on the left of the Welcome window. From here you can also open your mail, calendar, and To Do list (just as you can by clicking a hotspot). Bookmark buttons link to databases, bookmark pages, or even Web pages. Bookmark buttons are customizable; you learn how to add bookmarks throughout this book. Table 1.3 describes the default bookmark buttons that are found on the Welcome page.

TABLE 1.3   The Default Bookmark Bar Buttons

Click Here	To
	Open your **Mail** database. From here you can view your Inbox, create new mail, and so forth. You learn about the mail database in Lessons 2–5.
	Open the **Calendar** where you manage your appointments, access the calendars or free time of other people (given permission, of course), invite people to meetings, accept invitations, and so forth. You learn about calendar functions in Lessons 8–10.
	Opens your Address Book, where you keep information about your contacts.
	Open your **To Do** list. You learn how to work with To Do tasks in Lesson 11, "Working with To-Do Items."
	Open the **Replicator** page, which is the tool you use when you are working from a remote location or disconnected from the server. Learn about the Replicator page in Lesson 19, "Using Notes Remotely."
	Open the **Favorites Bookmarks** page. Favorites contains links to the databases and pages you visit frequently, such as your mail, address book, calendar, To Do list, and the Replicator Page (if you are a mobile user). Databases you visited recently also have bookmarks here.
	Open the **Databases** bookmark page. If you upgraded to Notes 6, all the databases you had on your workspace now appear on this bookmark page. To add a new bookmark to the page, drag the task button onto

TABLE 1.3   (continued)

Click Here	To
	the bookmark page. To remove a bookmark from a page, right-click the bookmark and select **Remove Bookmarks**.
	Open the **More Bookmarks** bookmark page, where you add any additional bookmarks that you want to use.
	Opens your **History** page, where you can see Internet pages and database pages you've previously viewed. If you are opening Notes for the first time, this folder will not contain any Internet pages.
	Open the **Internet Explorer** page. If you have Internet Explorer installed, the bookmarks for the Web browser appear here. If you have **Netscape Navigator** installed, the bookmarks for the Netscape Navigator appear here. If you have both of these programs installed, you see one bookmark for each program.

When a bookmark opens a task such as a database, a document, or mail, it opens the task in a new window and creates a new task button (see Figure 1.2). Opening a new window for each task is similar to the way a word processing document works—it opens a new window for each document you have open, or for each document you are creating. To move from window to window, click on the task button. In Figure 1.2, several tasks are open and several task buttons are displayed. Each task button contains a close button. Close a task by clicking the close button.

To create a bookmark from a task, drag the task onto the Bookmark bar or into a folder that is located on the bookmark bar. You can also create a bookmark for files on your PC such as Word documents or Excel spreadsheets by dragging the file from the file system to the bookmark bar.

Task buttons   Close task

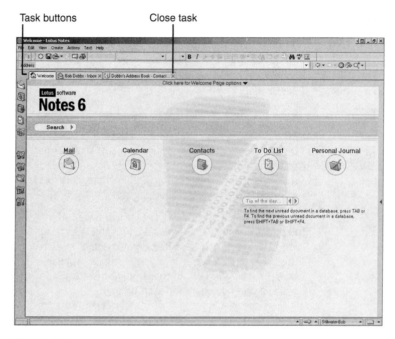

FIGURE 1.2
Here, the Welcome Page is the active page. Note that the Welcome task button is highlighted. Other open tasks include the Inbox, Calendar, Journal, and Address Book, all of which are represented with task buttons. Task buttons are also referred to as window tabs.

USING TOOLBARS

Some people prefer to click on buttons to perform program functions in lieu of accessing the menu. Like most programs that are designed to run under Microsoft Windows, buttons can be found on the window's toolbar. Toolbars are context sensitive, and they change depending upon the task you are performing in Notes. For example, one set of buttons appears when you are reading a document, and another set appears when you are editing a document. You can turn off context-sensitive toolbars (although we don't recommend it) by choosing

File, **Preferences**, **Toolbar Preferences**, and then turning off the
Show Context Sensitive Toolbar check box.

When you hold a mouse over one of the toolbar buttons, a brief
description of the icon appears. You learn how to customize, change
the position of, and create sets of Toolbars in Lesson 20,
"Customizing Notes."

USING DIALOG AND PROPERTIES BOXES

Often, selecting a menu command causes Notes to display a dialog
box, and right-clicking an item usually presents a menu from which
one can choose **Properties**. Dialog boxes and Properties boxes function similarly in that they both enable you to set options and make
specific choices related to the object with which you are currently
working. Each type of box contains certain elements that you need to
understand in order to use it.

Figure 1.3 shows a sample dialog box. The User Preferences dialog
box, which you access by choosing **File**, **Preferences**, **User
Preferences** from the menu, contains many of the elements common
to Notes dialog boxes. In fact, many of the elements are common to
Windows dialog boxes, as dialog boxes are really an element found in
all products designed to run in Windows. Table 1.4 describes those
elements and explains how to use them.

TABLE 1.4   Dialog Box Elements

Element	Description
Title bar	Indicates the name of the dialog box (such as the Open Database dialog box).
Drop-down list box	Displays one option from a list; click the arrow to the right of the box, and the box drops down to display the entire list.
List box	Displays a list of options so that you can see more than one choice at a time.

TABLE 1.4   (continued)

Element	Description
Scroll bar	Enables you to display additional items in a window or list box; click the up or down arrow to see more.
Text box	Allows you to enter a selection by typing it in the box.
Command button	Completes the commands or leads to another related dialog box that contains more options.
Close (X) button	Closes the dialog box without saving changes.
Check boxes	Provides selection or deselection of options individually; when the option is selected, a check mark appears in a small square box beside the option.
Radio buttons	(Not shown in figure) Provides selection or deselection from a group of options. Unlike check boxes, where you can select more than one option, radio buttons allow you to select only one option.
Check list	Enables you to select one or more items from a displayed list of options; click an option to select or deselect it, and a check mark appears beside it or disappears, respectively.

To use a dialog box, make your selections, as described in Table 1.4, and then choose a command button. The following list describes the functions of the most common command buttons:

- **OK** or **Done**—Accepts and puts into effect the selections you've made in the dialog box, and then closes the dialog box. Pressing the Enter key on your keyboard usually has the same effect as clicking the OK or Done button.

- **Cancel**—Cancels the changes you've made in the dialog box and closes it (as does the Close [X] button at the right end of the title bar).

- **Browse**—Browse (or any other button with an ellipsis following the button's name) displays another dialog box.

- **Open**—Open (or any other button with only a command on it) performs that command.

- **Help**—Displays information about the dialog box and its options.

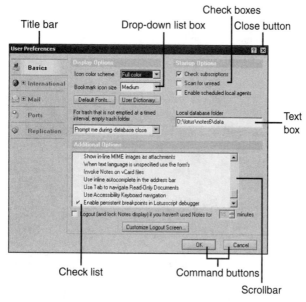

FIGURE 1.3
Use dialog boxes to make additional choices related to the selected menu command.

 I CAN'T GET RID OF THE DIALOG BOX!

After you've opened a dialog box, you must cancel or accept the changes you've made and close that dialog box before you can continue to work in Notes. Use the command buttons or the Close (**X**) button to close the dialog box.

Like a dialog box, a Properties box also presents options that are related to the menu commands. However, you work with a Properties box in a different way than you work with a dialog box. A Properties box displays only the properties of a specific item, such as selected text or a database. Properties contain information about an item such as its name, location, settings, design, size, and so on. When you make a selection in a Properties box, it takes effect immediately—even though the Properties box remains onscreen as you work.

Properties boxes contain tabbed pages that offer various options for the item you have selected. Figure 1.4 shows the properties box for selected text in a document.

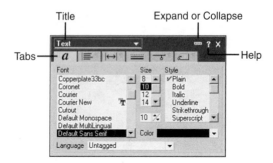

FIGURE 1.4
Use a Properties box to change the properties or attributes of selected items.

Properties boxes have many of the same elements that dialog boxes have: drop-down lists, list boxes, text boxes, and check boxes, for example. However, Properties boxes also contain the additional elements described in Table 1.5.

TABLE 1.5   Properties Box Elements

Element	Description
Title of Properties Box	The Properties box title displays the item for the properties shown, as in *Document* or *Text*. To change the item in the Properties box, use the drop-down list in the title bar.

TABLE 1.5   (continued)

Element	Description
Tabs	Named flaps that represent pages of options related to the selected element.
Help	Click this button to launch context-sensitive help.

Because a Properties box can remain onscreen while you work, you might want to reposition it on your screen. To move a Properties box, click the title bar and drag it to a new position.

COLLAPSE AND EXPAND

Click the **Collapse** icon on the title bar of a Properties box to collapse it. Collapsing hides all but the title bar and the tabs, and it frees up space on the workspace. When the box is collapsed, the icon becomes the Expand icon. Click the **Expand** icon to expand the Properties box back to its original view and size.

CHANGING AND LOCKING YOUR PASSWORD

The first time you use Lotus Notes, your system administrator will supply a password for you to use. You want to change your password so that no one else can access your mail and other databases. The ability to access information in Notes is based upon the use of your password and a file stored on your computer called your UserID file. To access information in Notes, a user needs both knowledge of the password and a copy of the UserID file on their computer. The UserID file is discussed in Appendix A, "Understanding Security and Access Rights." Here, we discuss changing and locking your password.

A password can have any combination of keyboard characters, as long as the first character is alphanumeric and you don't use spaces. Be careful when capitalizing your password, because Notes passwords are *case sensitive*, and *PASSWORD* is different from *password*.

Use the following steps to change your password:

1. Choose **File**, **Security**, **User Security** from the menu.

2. Enter your current password in the box (see Figure 1.5) and click OK.

FIGURE 1.5
As you enter your password, you see a series of X's.

3. When the User Security dialog box appears(see Figure 1.6), click **Change Password**.

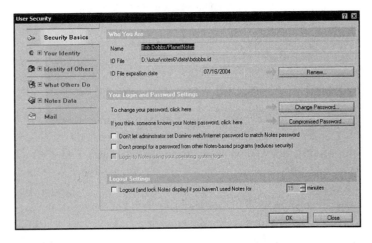

FIGURE 1.6
The User Security dialog box is where you set many of your user preferences in Notes. When changing your password, keep in mind that your password requires a minimum of eight characters and no spaces. Also remember that your password is case sensitive.

4. Enter your current password and click **OK**.

5. In the Change Password dialog box, enter your new password. You'll have to enter this new password twice. Be sure to type it correctly because you can't see the characters you type.

6. Click **Generate Password**.

7. If the password you create is not considered a good choice by Notes, you will see the Generate Password dialog box (see Figure 1.7) that allows you to select from a list of randomly created passwords. This is Notes way of letting you know that the password you chose is one which might be easy for hackers or others to guess. Click **OK** to close the User ID dialog box.

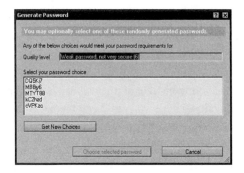

FIGURE 1.7
A good choice for a password uses upper- and lowercase, alpha and numeric characters. It should also be a word not found in the dictionary; for example "wildcat" is not a good choice for a password.

Always protect your password. Don't share it with anyone, and don't write reminders to yourself that you leave in obvious places (such as the Post-It note on your monitor).

SOMEONE IS ACCESSING MY MAIL!
Don't give your password to others, and never give your UserID file to others! If someone copies your UserID file, changing your password will not stop him from accessing your mail because the password is stored in the UserID file. For further security, it's also a good idea to change the password that was assigned to you by your Notes administrator. Typically, the administrator assigns a password that is easy for him (and you) to remember so that you can get up and running on Notes. It's not unusual for that password to be the same password that is assigned to all Notes users. Shortly after you become familiar with Notes, take the time to change your password—and keep it to yourself!

LOCKING YOUR ID

When you start Lotus Notes you enter your password. Once your password has been entered and authenticated by Notes, you can leave Notes running on your computer and you won't be prompted to enter your password again—unless you close and reopen Notes. If you walk away from your desk with Lotus Notes running, you stand the risk of others accessing your personal information and your mail. You may want to lock your ID in Notes, which will require you to reenter your password after a certain (determined by you) amount of time.

To lock your ID, choose **File**, **Security**, **Lock Display** from the menu, or press **F5**. Lotus Notes will display a large splash screen and no one can see your mail or other databases unless they enter your password. If you keep Notes open all day and you work with sensitive data or are in a high-traffic area, you can set Notes to automatically lock your ID for you after a specified time period of inactivity. To set up this automatic lock, choose **File**, **Preferences**, **User Preferences** from the menu to open the User Preferences dialog box. Enter the number of minutes in the Logout (and lock Notes display) if you haven't used

Notes for ____ Minutes. Click the checkbox in front of this field and enter your preferred number of minutes. Click **OK**. You can customize the logout screen as described in Lesson 20.

EXITING NOTES

When you're finished with Notes, you can close the program in several different ways:

- Choose **File**, **Exit Notes**.
- Double-click the application's Control menu button.
- Click the application's Control menu button, and choose **Close** from the menu.
- Press **Alt+F4**.
- Click the Close (**X**) button at the right end of the Notes title bar.

In this lesson, you learned how to start Notes, navigate the Notes window, use dialog boxes and Properties boxes, change your password, and exit Notes. In the next lesson you learn about reading mail.

LESSON 2
Reading Mail

In this lesson, you learn to open your mail inbox, select and read messages, use the preview pane, and close the mailbox.

OPENING YOUR MAIL INBOX

Mail, like all information found in Lotus Notes, is stored in a database. The stored mail includes copies of messages you've received and sent, as well as some specialized documents such as calendar entries and tasks. To open your mail database, click on the mail hotspot on the Welcome page or click the **Mail** bookmark.

When you first open a Lotus Notes database (such as Mail), the display is split into two large panes called the Navigation Pane and the View Pane. The titles of the available views are displayed in the pane on the left (the Navigation Pane), and more specific information is displayed in the pane on the right (the View Pane) .

THE NAVIGATION PANE

The Mail Navigation Pane (see Figure 2.1) lists views such as the Inbox, Drafts, Sent, and Trash, as well as Views, Folders, and Tools.

RESIZING THE PANES
You can change the size of the Navigation and View panes to see more of one side or the other. Point to the line that separates the two panes until your mouse pointer turns into a two-headed arrow, separated by a

black line. Drag that line to the left or right. You can
also resize the columns in the View pane. Use the
method that was just described for resizing panes, but
drag the lines between columns.

Views   Incoming mail   Action bar

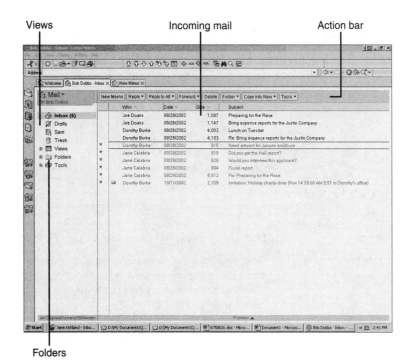

Folders

FIGURE 2.1
The Mail Navigation Pane with the Inbox view selected.

THE VIEW PANE

As you make choices in the Navigation Pane, documents change in
the View Pane. For example, when you click on Inbox, your incoming
mail messages are visible in the View Pane. When you click on the
Sent, however, your outbound mail messages are visible.

Click on the Inbox view to see your incoming mail messages. You can see who sent the message, the date it was sent, and the size and subject of the message. All unread messages have a red star in the selection bar to the left of the message (see Figure 2.1).

NO MAIL?

If you don't see mail, make sure that you have clicked the Inbox at the top of the Navigation Pane. If you are new to Notes, it's entirely possible that no mail has been sent to you, so no documents are listed in the View Pane.

Table 2.1 describes the views that are found in the Mail Navigation pane.

TABLE 2.1   Mail Database Views

View	Description
Inbox	Displays mail that has been sent to you.
Drafts	Stores mail messages you've elected to save as drafts instead of sending, which allows you to edit or make changes to the message before you send it.
Sent	Stores copies of messages you have sent if you choose to keep a copy of the message when you sent it.
Trash	Holds messages that are marked for deletion until you empty the trash or permanently delete the message.
Views	Click the + sign next to Views to access the All Documents and Discussion Thread views as described below.

TABLE 2.1 (continued)

View	Description
All Documents	(Available when you click the + next to Views)Displays all messages, including those you've sent, received, saved in folders, saved as drafts, and so on.
Discussion Threads	(Available when you click the + next to Views)A list of mail messages organized by conversation, with an initial message listed first and the responses to that message listed directly below it.
Folders	Contains the folders that you create to organize your mail. When you first open Lotus Notes, this folder is empty. Learn more about creating and using folders in Lesson 4, "Managing Mail."
Tools	Click the + sign next to the Tools icon to reveal the Archive, Rules and Stationery views.
Archive	Contains a view of documents that have been archived, or saved in a way that compacts the size of the database. Archiving is beyond the scope of this book; however, we recommend you read the Lotus Notes Help database regarding archiving and discuss archive settings and preferences with your System Administrator.
Rules	Displays a list of mail rules you have created. When you first open Lotus Notes, this view shows no rules. Learn more about rules in Lesson 5, "Using Mail Tools."
Stationery	Displays a list of custom stationery you have created and saved. If you are new to Notes, this shows no stationery. You learn more about stationery in Lesson 6.

DISCUSSION THREADS?

The Discussion Thread view is one of the most useful, yet most overlooked views in Lotus Notes. It can help you to determine if you've responded to an email, or if someone has responded to an email you sent to them. But it's important to understand that the Discussion Thread will only work when you answer an email using the "reply" feature and your mail recipients use the "reply" feature when answering your email. Replying to mail is discussed in Lesson 3, "Creating and Sending Mail."

THE ACTION BAR

The Action bar (see Figure 2.1) contains command buttons to assist you with your current task. For example, when you select a mail message in the View Pane, you can click one of these buttons to delete a message or to reply to a message. Like the menu bar and toolbars, the Action bar buttons change depending on in the task you are performing.

SELECTING AND MARKING MAIL

Before you can read, delete, print, or take any other action on a mail message, you must first *select* it. One message is already selected when you open your mailbox. To select a message, click once on the message in the View Pane. A selected message has a heavy black rectangle around the name, date, and subject of the message.

To select a different message in the list, click on it or use the up and down arrows on your keyboard to move to it. To select multiple messages, click in the column to the left of the "Who" column. This places a checkmark in that column; then any action you take will be applied to all checked documents, such as clicking the Delete button or the Print button.

You can also use the menu command **Edit, Select All** to select all the messages in the view, and you can use **Edit, Deselect All** to remove all the checkmarks from the messages in the view.

If you accidentally select a document, you can deselect it by clicking on the check mark again.

WHAT A DRAG!

If you want to select multiple messages, place your mouse cursor in the selection bar to the left of the messages. Click and hold down the mouse button and drag down the selection bar. This places check marks next to all the messages you drag past. You can deselect messages the same way.

READING AND PREVIEWING YOUR MAIL

To read a mail message, double-click the message or press the **Enter** key on a selected message. Figure 2.2 shows an open mail message.

Every mail message, or memo, contains the following elements:

- **Heading**—The heading contains the name of the person who sent the message, as well as the date and time it was sent. In addition, if you're on a Windows NT network, you might see the domain name, company name, or other information next to the sender's name.

- **To:**—The To: line shows the name of the person to whom the message is being sent. Again, the domain name might be included. If the message is coming to you, your name is displayed in the To: line.

- **cc:**—The cc: (carbon copy) line displays a list of anyone who received a copy of the message, as determined by the sender.

- **bcc:**—The bcc: (blind carbon copy) line contains a list of anyone who received a blind copy of the message, as determined by the sender; however, only the sender sees the entire contents of the bcc: field. For example, if Jane sends an email and lists Dorothy and Rob in the bcc: field, Dorothy will see only her name in that field, and Rob will see only his name in the field, but Jane (the originator of the email) sees both names in that field.

- **Subject**—The subject describes the topic of the message, as defined by the sender of the message.

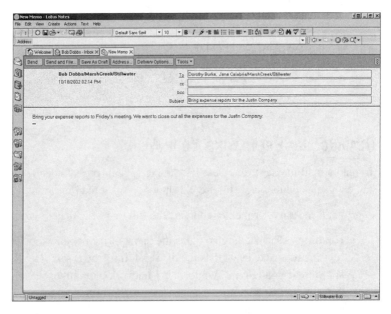

FIGURE 2.2
Messages display in the Mail Memo form.

The rest of the email message form is the body field. The mail body field in Lotus Notes is a *rich text field*, which means that you can read and create text with attributes such as bold and italics, and you can view and create images in your email. If you cannot view an entire message onscreen at once, use the vertical scroll bar, or use the Page Up, Page Down, and arrow keys on your keyboard to navigate.

SHORTCUTS

You can press **Ctrl+End** to go to the end of a long message or **Ctrl+Home** to go to the beginning of a message.

PLAIN ENGLISH

Rich Text Field

Information that is stored in Lotus Notes is stored in fields. A *rich text field* is the only type of field that can accept multiple data types: text, numbers, graphics, file attachments, and so forth. It is also the only kind of field in which you can assign text and paragraph attributes such as changing the font, bolding or italicizing text, or changing the spacing between paragraphs and creating numbered lists.

When you finish reading a message, press the **Esc** key to return to your Inbox, or click on the **X** at the top right of the message task button.

UNDERSTANDING READ MARKS

You can tell at a glance of your Inbox which messages you've read and which you haven't read, or opened. Mail messages you haven't read appear in red and have a red star located in the selection bar to the left of the mail message. After you open and read the message, the star disappears, and the mail message appears in black. Figure 2.3 shows both read and unread messages in the Inbox, as well as messages that are marked, or selected.

USING THE PREVIEW PANE

The *Preview pane* enables you to read most of your messages from the Inbox view without opening them in a new window. To see the

Preview pane, click on the Preview triangle at the bottom of your
View Pane (see Figure 2.4).

Marked messages
    Selection bar

Unread marks

FIGURE 2.3
*Red stars display in your Inbox indicating which messages have not been
opened (read), and checkmarks appear next to messages that have been
marked, or selected.*

Once the Preview Pane is open, you can resize it by placing your cursor at the top of the pane, and when the cursor turns into a double-
headed arrow, drag the mouse up or down the screen to obtain the size
pane you prefer.

With the Preview Pane open, the Inbox view is now split into three
panes, as shown in Figure 2.5.

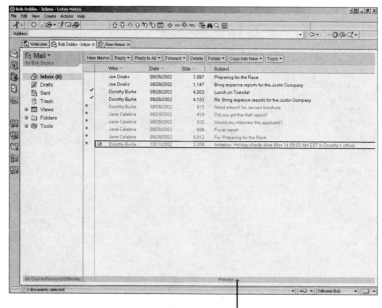

Click here to open Preview pane

FIGURE 2.4
The Preview pane triangle is new in Lotus Notes 6. In previous versions, the pre-view pane was available, but this version makes accessing the pane much easier by placing this triangle at the bottom of your View Pane.

With the Preview pane activated, the mail message that is selected in the View pane is the message that displays in the Preview pane. To navigate through mail while using the Preview pane, you can do the following:

- Use the up and down arrow keys on your keyboard

- Use the Navigation SmartIcons on the toolbar

- Use your mouse to select a mail message

Previous ┐ ┌ Next Unread
      Next ┐ ┌ Previous Unread

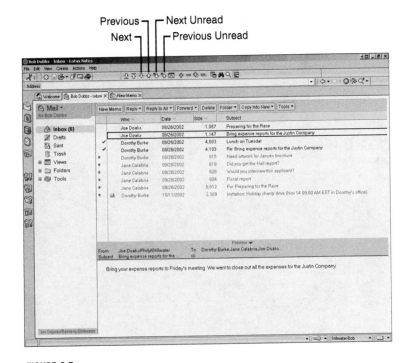

FIGURE 2.5
The Preview pane enables you to read most mail messages quickly. If you prefer, press the Enter key to view your mail message, and use the navigator buttons on the toolbar to navigate through your mail.

PREVIEWING IS NOT READING

By default, Lotus Notes does not consider previewed mail as having been read. Unread marks continue to display until you open individual mail messages. You can change this default setting but be warned; by changing the default if you use your keyboard arrow keys to quickly pass over messages in your inbox, each one you pass will be marked as "read" even though you didn't take the time to read the actual message, but merely cursored over it. To change this default, choose **File, Preferences, User Preferences** from the menu. In the **Additional Options** box, place a check mark next to **Mark documents read when opened in preview pane**. Click **OK**.

In this lesson, you learned how to open and close your mail database, and how to read and navigate your incoming mail messages. In the next lesson, you learn to create and send mail.

Lesson 3

Creating and Sending Mail

In this lesson, you learn to create, send, reply to, and forward an email message. You also learn how to select, copy, and move text; to set delivery options; and to save mail messages as drafts.

Opening a New Mail Memo

Notes mail messages use a form called the Mail Memo form (see Figure 3.1) and can contain formatted text, tables, graphics, attachments, graphs, and embedded objects.

You can create mail messages from any area of Notes, even when you are working in other databases. Use one of the following methods to create a mail message from your Inbox:

- Click the **New Memo** button on the Action bar.

- Choose **Create**, **Memo** from the menu.

A blank memo like the one in Figure 3.1 appears. Your name and today's date and time are displayed in the Heading of the email. A separate task button labeled New Memo displays to the right of the Inbox. The message is split into two parts: The *heading* is the top part and the *body* is the bottom.

Filling in the Heading

The heading of the mail memo consists of fields; you begin your email by filling out those fields. Follow these steps to complete the heading information:

Body   Filled in by Notes if you pressed the Reply button   Heading

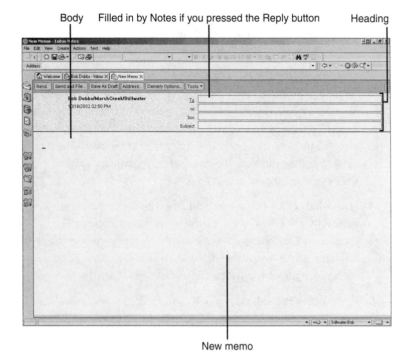

New memo

FIGURE 3.1
To display a new Memo like the one shown here, click the New Memo button on the Action bar. If you are responding to an email in your Inbox, click the Reply button, which will also display a new mail memo but with the To: field filled in.

1. Type the name of the person to whom you want to send the memo in the **To** field. To send to multiple recipients, separate the names in the **To** field with a comma.

2. As you type, Notes searches your personal address book and a companywide address book called the "Directory" to find a match for the name you are typing. This feature, called quick-address, continues to search as you type until it finds the unique name you want. Quick-address searches for both first names and last names. If you don't like this feature, it

can be disabled in the Mail section of your Location document. See "Creating Location Documents" in Lesson 19, "Using Notes Remotely," for more information.

3. **(Optional)** Use the Tab key or your mouse to move to the **cc** (carbon copy) field. Type the name of the person to whom you want to send a copy of the message. The cc field is used to send a copy of a message to someone who is not directly affected by the message, but who needs to know about the contents of the message for informational purposes only. Quick-address works in this field, too.

4. **(Optional)** Click in the **bcc** field and type the name of the person to whom you want to send a blind carbon copy. The recipients of the message, and those listed in the carbon copy field, do not know that the person who is listed in the blind carbon copy field received a copy of the message.

5. In the **Subject** field, enter a descriptive title for your message. It is extremely important that you fill in a Subject because it appears in the recipients' Inbox views, telling them the purpose of your message. To create multiple lines within the subject line, press the **Enter** key.

ALWAYS FILL IN THE SUBJECT LINE

Don't send email without including a clear and concise description of your message in the Subject line. It lets your recipients know what the message is about before they open it. If you enter something benign like "read this!" you are taking the chance that people will not read (or even delete without reading) your message, as they may think it's an advertisement or junk mail. Be descriptive and professional, and by helping the recipient determine the contents of your mail without opening it, you are helping yourself to ensure your email will be read.

USING ADDRESS BOOKS

Most Notes clients have two *address books*: the *Personal Address Book*, which is usually stored on your local hard drive, and at least one of the *Directories* stored on the Domino server. Like everything else in Notes and Domino, these address books are databases. You are the only person who has access to your personal address book, and your last name is usually part of the database name (for example, "Burke's Address Book"). The Directory is accessible to everyone in your company and it usually contains the name of your company (for example, "Rockteams Address Book") in the title. The Directory is managed by your company's system administrators; you manage the content of your Personal Address Book.

While you're writing a memo, you can use the address books to add people to your **To, cc**, and **bcc** fields. This is especially useful if you aren't sure of a person's last name or the spelling of his name. Use the following steps to access the address books from a new mail memo:

1. Click the **Address** button on the Action bar. The Select Addresses dialog box appears, as shown in Figure 3.2. Table 3.1 lists the options in this dialog box.

2. Select the address book you want to access. If you are using the Notes client for the first time, your Personal Address Book is probably empty at this point, but it can be easily populated using the Copy Local button. In order to access the companywide Directory, you have to connect to the Domino server.

3. Select the names of the individuals or groups from the available list of names. To select one person, click on that person's name; to select more than one person, click once in the margin to the left of the person's name to place a checkmark next to their name.

4. Click on **To, cc**, or **bcc**, depending on which address field you want to complete. Or you can click the **Copy Local** button to add this person or people to your personal address book.

5. Click **OK**.

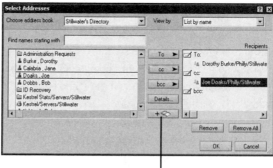

Add to Local button

FIGURE 3.2
Choose your address book and mail recipients in the Select Addresses dialog box. To add a person to your Personal Address Book at the same time as you are using this dialog box to address mail, click the Add Local Button.

TABLE 3.1   The Select Addresses Dialog Box

Prompt	Description
Choose Address Book	The names of all the address books to which you have access.
Find Names Starting with	Type in the first letter of the name you are looking for to jump to the names that begin with that letter. As you continue to type, Notes narrows suggested entries with each letter you enter. So, if you type J, you'll see names that begin with J; if you type Ja, you'll see names that begin with Ja; and so forth.
View by	Pull-down choices enable you to change the order of the display of the names in the address books. The default setting is List by Name. Other choices include by Notes name hierarchy, Corporate hierarchy, and categorized by language.

TABLE 3.1   (continued)

Prompt	Description
Details	Opens up the Person Document in the Directory, where additional information is stored about the individual. If you select a group, the members of the group are displayed.
To>, cc>, bcc>	Fills in the heading fields with the names that are selected.
Remove, Remove All	Removes either just the selected names, or all the names from the Recipients window.

COMPLETING THE MESSAGE

Type the message you want to send in the lower half of the screen, which is known as the *body* (see Figure 3.1). Unlike the fields in the heading, the text and the paragraphs in the body of the message can be formatted, because this is a *rich text field*. You learn more about rich text formatting in Lesson 15, "Editing and Formatting Text and Fields," and more about attachments in Lesson 17, "Working with Attachments."

USING SPELL CHECK

Spell Check compares your text against a stored spelling dictionary of tens of thousands of words. If any of your words aren't in the spelling dictionary, Spell Check tells you that the word is possibly misspelled. In addition to your misspellings and typos, Spell Check also alerts you to proper names and unusual words that might be spelled correctly, but that are not in the spelling dictionary.

Lotus Notes looks in two dictionaries for correctly spelled words. The main dictionary is extensive, covering most of the common words in American English. Proper names, acronyms, and business jargon that are not included in the main dictionary are then looked for in your user dictionary. The user dictionary is one to which you can add words.

Spell Check reports duplicate words, such as *the the*, but it won't look at single-character words such as *a* or *I*, or words that are longer than 64 letters. It also ignores text that doesn't have any letters, such as the number 1,200,543.

Unlike other programs, for example some word processing programs, Spell Check does not operate on-the-fly. When you want to check the spelling in your message, you must be in edit mode. Edit mode enables you to change the text in the document in which you are currently working. When you're *creating* a new mail message, you're automatically in edit mode.

To run Spell Check, follow these steps:

1. Choose **Edit, Check Spelling**, or, if you have toolbars displayed, click the **Check Spelling** button. If Spell Check finds a questionable word, the Spell Check dialog box appears, as shown in Figure 3.3.

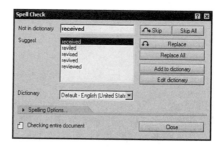

FIGURE 3.3
From the Spell Check dialog box, you can add new entries to your personal dictionary, correct spelling errors, and skip words.

2. When Spell Check finds a word it doesn't recognize, the word appears in the **Replace** box of the dialog box. You can then choose one of the following options:

- **Skip**—Ignores the misspelling and goes on to the next word. Use this option when the word is spelled correctly.

- **Skip All**—Tells Notes to ignore all the instances of this word in the message. This is useful when a correctly spelled proper name crops up several times in a memo.

- **Replace**—Enables you to change an incorrect spelling to a correct one. If the correct spelling of the word shows up in the Guess box, click the correct guess and then the **Replace** button. If Spell Check provides no suggestions and you know the correct spelling, click in the **Not in dictionary** field and make the correction by deleting or adding characters. Then, click **Replace** to make the change in your message.

- **Replace All**—Tells Notes to replace all the instances of this word with the suggested word you choose.

- **Add to Dictionary**—Adds the selected word to your user dictionary. After the word is added, Spell Check recognizes it as correctly spelled.

- **Edit Dictionary**—Opens a new dialog box displaying the contents of your personal dictionary. This is very useful when you accidentally add an incorrectly spelled word to your personal dictionary and need to correct or delete that word.

3. After correcting, adding, or replacing words that Lotus Notes Spell Check has questioned, click **Close**.

By default, Spell Check checks your entire mail message. If you want to Spell Check one word or a paragraph, select the word or text with your mouse, and then start the Spell Check using the previously outlined process. Running Spell Check doesn't guarantee a perfect mail message. If you accidentally type the word *form* when you wanted to type *from*, for example, Spell Check won't catch it because *form* is a word that is in the dictionary. Also, Spell Check doesn't catch incorrect punctuation or missing words.

As previously mentioned, you might mistakenly add a misspelled word to your personal dictionary. To edit your personal dictionary when not running spell check, do the following.

1. Choose **File**, **Preferences**, **User Preferences**. In the User Preferences dialog box (see Figure 3.4), click the plus mark next to **International** and click on **Spell Check**. On the right side of the dialog box, click the **Edit User Dictionary** button.

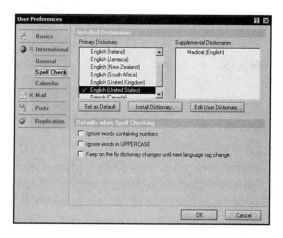

FIGURE 3.4
The User Preferences dialog box is where you can make changes to many of the default settings for Lotus Notes 6.

2. You can then make any of the following changes:

   • To delete the incorrectly spelled word, select it and click **Delete**.

   • To change a misspelled word, select it from the list, enter the correct spelling in the small text box at the bottom of the dialog box, and then click **Update**.

- To add a word, enter it in the small text box and click **Add**.

3. When you finish, click **OK**. Then, click **OK** to close the User Preferences dialog box.

AUTOMATIC SPELL CHECKING

You can set a user preference to automatically perform a Spell Check on every mail message you create. It is highly recommended that you set this option. Open your mail database and choose **Tools, Preferences** from the Action bar. On the Basics tab of the Mail section, select **Automatically check mail messages for misspellings before sending**. Click **OK** to close the window.

SENDING MAIL

When you have completed spell check (see Figure 3.5), you can send the message or you can save it as a draft to send later.

To send the message, click the **Send** button or the **Send and File** button in the Action bar:

Send   Notes sends the message to the recipient's mailbox and, by default, saves a copy of your message in the Sent view.

Send and File   In addition to sending the message, you are given the option of storing a copy of the message in a folder. For more information about creating folders, see Lesson 4, "Managing Mail."

To save a message as a draft, click the **Save As Draft** button in the Action bar. Your message is stored in the Drafts folder. At a later time, you can open the message by double-clicking the message from the Drafts view. The document is automatically opened in edit mode. When you're ready to send the message choose **Send** or **Send and File** in the Action bar.

Send and File

Send | Save As Draft

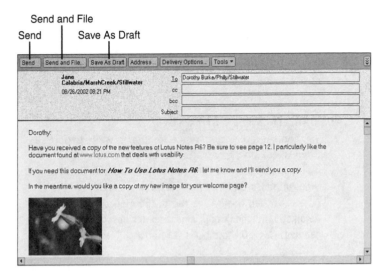

FIGURE 3.5
A completed message can be sent or saved in the drafts folder. The body of the message is a rich text field and can contain formatted text as shown here.

CHOOSING DELIVERY OPTIONS

You control how and when each of your mail messages is delivered through the **Delivery Options** button on the Action bar. Delivery Options, as described in Tables 3.2 and 3.3, have to be set prior to sending the message. If you are sending mail via the Internet to non-Notes users, some of these features do not work, and they are marked as such with an asterisk (*) in Tables 3.2 and 3.3.. See Figure 3.6 to see the Delivery Options dialog box, which appears when you click the Options button on the Action Bar. To learn more about Notes and Internet mail, refer to Que's *Special Edition Using Lotus Notes and Domino*.

IS THIS REALLY NECESSARY?

For the most part, you do not need to access Delivery Options for each mail memo you send. The default settings in Notes may be sufficient for efficient sending and receiving of mail. Changing the priority of a mail memo can affect the performance of your Domino servers. Discuss mail delivery options with your supervisor, help desk, or system administrator and ask them to suggest if and when you need to set or change your email delivery options.

TABLE 3.2   Basic Delivery Options

Option	Description
*Importance	Choices: Normal, High, or Low. If this is set to High, an exclamation mark appears to the left of the message in the recipient's Inbox. The envelope icon to the left of the message in the sender's Sent view is red. Otherwise, no icon appears.
Delivery report	Tells Notes to place a report in your mailbox that indicates how the delivery of your message went. The default option is Only on Failure. Your system administrator might ask you to change this option if you are experiencing mail problems. Otherwise, there is no need to change this option.
Delivery priority	Marks the message as Normal, High, or Low priority. Priority governs how quickly the mail is delivered. When you send a message to a recipient on the same Domino server, it is not necessary to choose a priority—Normal priority delivers it immediately. When you send a Notes message to a different Domino server or to the Internet, High priority causes your Domino server to deliver it immediately, instead of at the

TABLE 3.2   (continued)

Option	Description
	scheduled delivery set by your system administrator. Low priority means that the mail will be delivered in the middle of the night, during off-business hours.
Return receipt	Places a receipt in your mail Inbox that tells you the time and date at which the recipient received the message.
*Prevent copying	Prevents the recipient from forwarding, copying, or printing your message. Use this if the information is highly confidential.
Auto Spellcheck	Automatically spell checks the mail memo you are sending.
Do not notify me recipient(s) are running out of office	When a Notes user is using the Out of Office feature of Notes, automatic replies are generated to each sender when this person receives mail. If you check this box in your preferences, Notes will reject any automatic Out of Office replies that would come to you as a response to the mail memo you are sending.
Sign	Adds a unique digital code to your message that identifies you as the sender.
Encrypt	Encodes the message so that no one but the intended recipient can read it.
Save these security	Click this box and the Sign and Encrypt options as the default options you have chosen will be saved as the default for all of your mail messages.
*Mood stamp	Mood stamps create graphics that appear in the Inbox of other Lotus Notes mail users. To add a mood stamp, select one from the pull-down list. Mood stamps will appear in the box below the pull-down list as you select them, enabling you to see the graphic that will appear in the recipients Inbox.

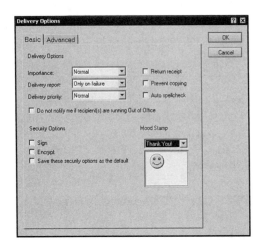

FIGURE 3.6
Set your delivery preferences in the Delivery Options dialog box. Please check with your Domino System Administrator before you send mail High priority. It might not be necessary for you to select that option for important mail.

PLAIN ENGLISH

Encrypt

Sounds like you need to put on your magic decoder ring! When you choose to encrypt a message, Lotus Notes scrambles the message, and only the recipient has the key to unscramble it. Because your message travels from your PC to the Lotus Notes server and then to the PC of the recipient, encrypting the message prevents anyone who might be working at the Lotus Notes server from reading your message.

WHY IS HE MAD AT ME?

Lots of new Notes users think that the Flame mood stamp indicates that a message is "hot" (important). In the true Net Etiquette sense, flaming is an indicator that

you are truly angry with someone, and is considered
insulting. You might want to think twice about using this
mood stamp.

You can find less frequently used delivery mail options by choosing
the **Advanced** tab of the Delivery Options dialog box. For example,
you can set mail expiration dates and request where and when you
want replies to messages to be sent. Figure 3.7 shows the advanced
options for sending mail.

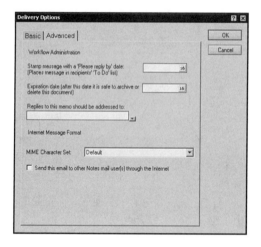

FIGURE 3.7
*The Advanced Delivery Options are not used as frequently as the Basic Delivery
Options. For most of your mail, you can leave these options set at their default
settings and you need not access this box.*

TABLE 3.3 Advanced Delivery Options

Option	Description
Stamp Reply by Date	Select the date from the calendar. The message is placed in the recipient's To

TABLE 3.3   (continued)

Option	Description
	Do list. It is also marked in the heading with the requested reply date.
Expiration date	Set Rules to automatically delete or archive mail messages based on an expiration date. More information on rules can be found in Lesson 5, "Using Mail Tools."
Send Replies to	Choose the individual to whom you want the replies to be sent. This is especially useful if you want someone else to manage the replies to a particular message.
MIME Character Set	Select the MIME character set you need to use when sending messages over the Internet. Unless your system administrator instructs you to change this, leave the setting as Default.
Sending Notes to Notes	Check this if you are sending to a Notes user over the Internet to ensure that Notes-centric formatting is preserved.

REPLYING TO MAIL

To reply to a mail message, select the message to which you want to reply in the view pane, or open the message. Click the **Reply** or the **Reply to All** button in the Action bar. Each of these buttons has the same choices on its pull-down menus, beginning with **Reply**. The difference between the two buttons is that the **Reply** button sends your reply to the sender only; the **Reply to All** button sends your reply to the sender and anyone he included in his to: and cc: fields.

Follow these steps to reply to mail:

1. Click the **Reply** or **Reply to All** button and choose Reply from the pull-down list. The New Reply window appears. When you reply to mail, Notes fills in the header information of your mail message. You can make changes to the header information if you want.

2. To send a carbon copy of the message to new parties, type the names in the **cc** field. If you used the Reply to All button and the sender had names in the cc: field, those names will be filled in.

   To send blind carbon copies, type the names in the **bcc** field.

3. Position the mouse cursor in the message body and begin typing your reply message.

4. Click the **Send** or **Send and File** button on the Action bar.

Use the **Reply with History** option to attach a copy of the original message to the bottom of the reply. Use this option when you want to respond to a lengthy message, providing the recipient with a copy of the original message, or when you just want to make it easy for the recipient to understand your reply by attaching their original email. Keep in mind that **Reply with History** will resend any attachments that you received in this email. If there were attachments in the email you received, you might want to choose the **Reply without Attachment(s)** option, which sends the body of the email but not the attachments.

Choose the Reply with **Internet Style History** if you are replying to an email you received from someone who is not using Lotus Notes. This options strips out headers from the original message as shown in Figure 3.8. This makes a much cleaner history and is easier for non-Notes users to read.

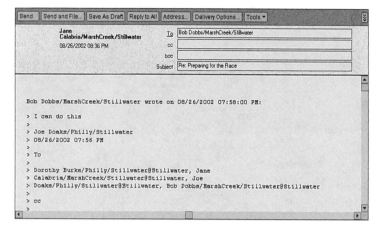

FIGURE 3.8
Using the Reply with Internet Style History results in a more compact and easier to read email memo for Internet mail users. Notice the line of text added by Notes, indicating the original author and date sent.

DON'T FORGET OTHERS!

Use the **Reply to All** button when replying to mail that originally included others in the header fields. This is a courtesy that saves you time later, when you discover that you have not informed everyone in the original distribution list of your reply.

FORWARDING MAIL

You can forward any mail message (that has not been restricted with the "Prevent copying" feature) to another person, and you even can add your own comments or reply to it. To pass a message on to someone else, click the **Forward** button in the Action bar. Options for this feature are **Forward without Attachments** and **Internet-Style Forward**. These options work similarly to the reply options discussed in the previous section, "Replying to Mail."

When you select a **Forward** option, the New Memo window appears (see Figure 3.9).

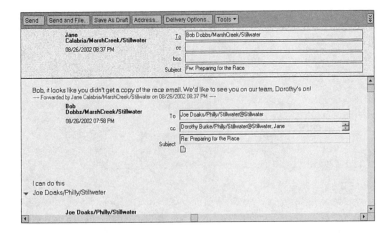

FIGURE 3.9
You can add comments to forwarded messages, explaining your purpose for sending this message.

Forwarding a mail message inserts one mail message into another so that the original header information stays intact. Complete the To: and Subject: lines and add your comments above the Forwarded by line. Click the **Send** or **Send and File** button in the Action bar to send the message.

CREATING A NEW MAIL MEMO FROM QUICK NOTES

Quick Notes is a new feature of Lotus Notes R6 and it enables you to quickly create a new mail memo, contact, journal entry, or reminder from the Welcome Page (see Figure 3.10). To enable Quick Notes, click the small blue triangle on the right side of your Welcome Page.

Place cursor in these fields to create a mail memo

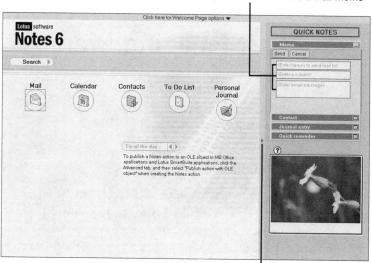

Close Quick Notes

FIGURE 3.10
To close Quick Notes, click the small blue triangle to the left of Quick Notes. Resize the Quick Notes window by dragging the left border of the Quick Notes frame.

To Create a new mail memo from Quick Notes, simply place your cursor in the To:, Subject:, and message fields and type your information.

In this lesson, you learned how to create, reply to, and send mail. You also learned how to use Spell Check and set delivery options, as well as use a new feature of Lotus Notes called Quick Notes. In the next lesson you learn how to sort, manage, and print mail.

LESSON 4
Managing Mail

In this lesson, you will learn to navigate through mail, sort messages, delete messages, use folders, and print mail.

NAVIGATING THROUGH MAIL

There are two ways to navigate through your Inbox. The first is by using your keyboard: Press the **Enter** key to open a message and press it again to read the next message, the **Backspace** key to read the previous message, or the **Esc** key to return to the Inbox view. Alternately, continue to read unopened (unread) messages using buttons on the toolbar. There are four buttons that help you navigate through your mail without returning to the Inbox:

Use the Navigate Next and Navigate Previous buttons (the plain up and down arrow icons on the toolbar) to navigate to the next or the previous mail message.

Use the Navigate Next Unread and Navigate Previous Unread buttons (the up and down arrows with stars on the toolbar) to navigate to the next or the previous unread message.

SORTING MAIL

By default, the Inbox view is sorted by date in ascending order, which means that the older messages are at the top of the view and the newer messages are at the bottom. You can change the sort order of the documents in a view by clicking on the view column headers. However, not all the columns in the view can be changed. You can tell *which* columns can be sorted by the triangle on the column head. The sortable column headers have triangles on them. For example, in the Inbox view, the Who column header has an up triangle that indicates that this column can be re-sorted in ascending order (alphabetically, from A–Z). The Date column has a down triangle, which means this column can be re-sorted in descending order (from most recent to oldest). The Size column has a down triangle, indicating that the messages can be re-sorted by size, with the largest messages first.

If the option to sort both ways is available in a view, there are two triangles in the column heading—one points up and the other points down. Once you sort columns, the columns stay in the sort order you placed them in, even if you exit Notes and open it again.

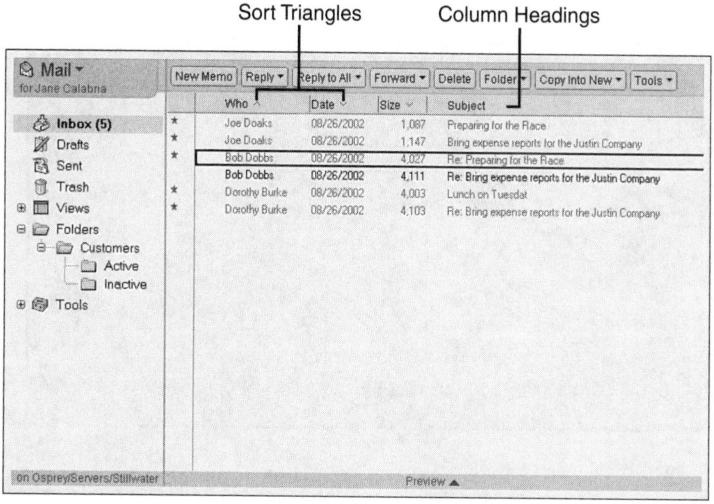

FIGURE 4.1
Sorting columns on-the-fly can help you find messages quickly.

DELETING MAIL

To keep your Mail database manageable, make it a practice to clear out old messages when you are through with them. "Read it and delete it" is a good practice and helps to keep your database file at a manageable size. If you think you'll need the message again, archive it or store it in a folder. If you know that you don't need the message anymore, delete it.

When you delete mail messages in Notes, they get moved to the Trash folder in your mail database. Deleted mail messages will stay in the Trash folder for a period of time that you designate. To set a time for deletion, open your Inbox and choose **Tools, Preferences**. Set the specified period of time as shown in Figure 4.2.

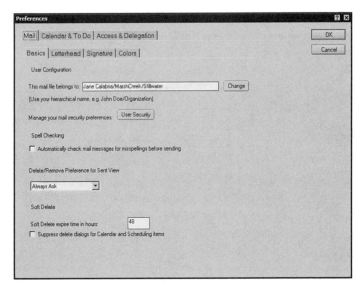

FIGURE 4.2
In previous chapters you accessed default settings and user preferences by choosing File, Preferences, User Preferences. But additional settings and mail preferences can be accessed from the Action bar in Mail by choosing Tools, Preferences.

You can mark messages for deletion while you're reading them, or you can do it from the view pane. Use the following steps to delete a message while you are in read mode:

1. In the opened message, click the **Delete** button on the Action bar or press the **Delete** key on your keyboard.

2. Lotus Notes marks your open message for deletion and closes the message; your next message appears.

3. Continue reading the rest of your messages, deleting those that you don't want to keep.

OOPS! CAN I GET THE MESSAGE BACK?

You can manually empty your Trash folder by clicking the Empty Trash button on the toolbar when you are in the Trash folder view. When you empty the trash can and confirm deletion of messages, they are *permanently* deleted from your mail database. You cannot get these messages back.

To mark messages for deletion while you are in the Inbox or while you are in some other view, you must first select the message or messages you want to delete. This can be done using one of the methods for selecting documents that were described in Lesson 2.

To permanently delete the message, open the **Trash** view in the Mail Navigator pane. You'll see the messages you marked for deletion in the View pane, as shown in Figure 4.3.

Click the **Empty Trash** button in the Action bar to delete messages in the Trash view. Alternately, to delete a single item, highlight the item and click **Delete Selected Item**.

CHANGE YOUR MIND?

If you decide that you do not want to permanently delete the message, you can click the **Restore** or **Restore All** buttons in the Action bar of the Trash view. The deletion marks that appear next to messages are then removed. Messages disappear from the Trash view at this point, but they are visible in their original view. When a message is restored into the Inbox, it is marked Unread so it will appear in red with a red start next to it.

ALL FOR ONE, ONE FOR ALL

A view is just a means of organizing the same set of messages in your mail database. Views are like templates: If you create a folder and move a document to that folder, the same document also shows up in your All Documents view. There aren't two copies of the document in your database, just two templates, or views, for accessing the document. Be careful! When you delete a message from *one* view, it is deleted from *all* views. See Lesson 6, "Working with Databases," for more information on views.

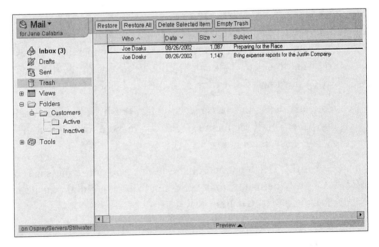

FIGURE 4.3
The Trash view displays messages that are marked for deletion in the View pane.

USING FOLDERS

Each time you select another view in the Mail Navigator pane, you see different documents in the View pane, or you see the same documents sorted in a different way. If you want to save a mail message, assign it to an existing folder by dragging it to that folder. Alternately, select the message and choose **Folder**, **Move to Folder** or **Remove from Folder** from the Action bar, and if moving to a folder, select a folder from the list of folders.

DELETING FROM FOLDERS

Be careful when deleting documents from your folders because this action deletes those documents from your mail database. When you place a document in a folder or folders, it does not make a new copy of the document for each location; you are actually creating a pointer to that one document in the database. If you no longer want a particular document in a folder, select it and click on **Folder** in the Action bar and then **Remove from Folder** from the pull-down list.

CREATING AND DELETING FOLDERS

You can create your own folders in which to save your mail. To create a folder, follow these steps:

1. Choose **Folder, Create Folder** from the Action bar.

2. In the Create Folder dialog box, type the name of the new folder directly over the word *Untitled* in the Folder name box. Figure 4.4 shows the **Create Folder** dialog box in which a folder is being created. When you open this dialog box, "Untitled" appears in the **Folder name** box until you replace it with your desired title.

3. The default folder type on the **Advanced** tab of this dialog box is **Shared**. Leave this default as your choice.

4. Select the location for the new folder. The default location is **Folders,** but you can place your new folder within an existing folder by selecting an existing folder. For example, create a folder called Customers, and then create two folders under Customers called Active and Inactive (see Figure 4.5).

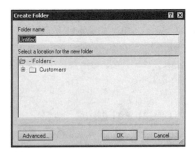

FIGURE 4.4
Type the name of your new folder in the Create Folder dialog box.

5. To select a design for your folder, click on the **Advanced** tab and click the **Copy From** button. The design determines how documents are viewed. By default, the design is the All Documents view, so the columns and headers you see in the All Documents view are the same columns and headers you will see in your new folder. However, only the documents you send to that folder will show when you open the folder. But you might want your new folder to look like your drafts folder, where the column header information differs from the Inbox folder. When you click the Copy From button, select a folder on which to base your new folder.

6. Click **OK** to save your changes and see your new folder in the Mail Navigator Pane (see Figure 4.5).

TIP

The newly created folder immediately appears in the Mail Navigator pane. You can open it at any time by clicking on it; its contents appear in the View pane. You also can move and add messages to folders by clicking and dragging selected documents to folders you have created.

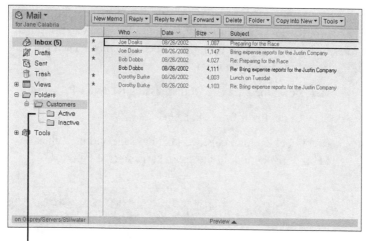

Nested folders

FIGURE 4.5
The Mail Navigator pane, showing nested custom folders.

We don't recommend you create a *private* folder. Any *shared* folder
you create in your Mail database is essentially private because it's part
of your mail database and protected by your password and userID. For
more information on private folders, consult the Lotus Notes Help
database or talk with your system administrator. To delete a folder,
remove it from the Navigation Pane by selecting it and choosing
Actions, **Folder Options**, **Remove Folder** from the menu (not the
Action bar). Any memos that are contained in the folder at the time
you delete the folder remain in the All Documents view of the Mail
database; they are not deleted when you delete the folder.

PRINTING MAIL

You can print one or many mail messages at a time, and as with many
Windows products, you can activate the Print command in several
ways. However, like deleting and moving documents, if you want to
print multiple messages you must first select the messages in the view

pane by placing a check mark in the selection bar to the left of the messages. If you want to print just one message, you can print that message from the view or from the opened document. Then print using one of the following methods:

- Hold down the **Ctrl** key while pressing the letter **P**.

- Select **File, Print** from the menu.

- Right-click on the unopened mail message and then click on **Print** at the bottom of the shortcut menu (see Figure 4.6).

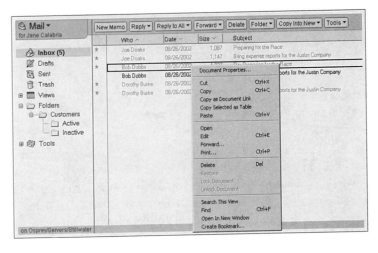

FIGURE 4.6
Right-click on the message to access the shortcut menu.

All three of the previous options present the Print dialog box (see Figure 4.7), which enables you to select the printer, print a view, print selected documents with various page break and form options, select the pages to print, and print multiple copies.

At times, it's useful to print a view. For example, you might want to print a list of your customer emails contained in your active customer folder (if you created such a folder). When you print a view, the information displayed is exactly as it is displayed in the view pane, and in the case of mail, it would show you the Who, Date, Size, and Subject fields. To print a view, choose **File, Print** from the menu. In the **What to Print** portion of the Print dialog box, click **Selected View**. Click **OK** to print.

When you choose the **Print** command, the Print View dialog box that is shown in Figure 4.7 appears. Table 4.1 describes the Print dialog box options in detail.

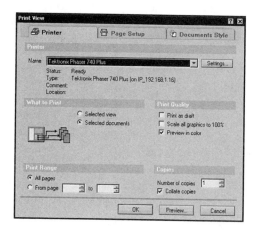

FIGURE 4.7

Set print options in the Print dialog box. Click the Settings button if you need to make changes such as selecting a particular tray, printing duplex, and so forth.

TABLE 4.1   Common Print Options

Option	Description
Printer	Use the drop-down menu to select your printer if you have the multiple printers installed.
What to Print	Choose Selected view to print the current view, or Selected documents to print documents you have selected or a single document which is selected.

TABLE 4.1   (continued)

Option	Description
Print range	Select All to print all pages of the message, or select From and To and enter the beginning and ending page numbers for the document you want to print.
Print quality	Choose the **Print as draft** option if you don't need a letter-quality copy (dark text and nice looking graphics). Draft quality enables the printer to print more quickly and uses toner more sparingly. This feature might not work on all printers. Choose **Scale all graphics to 100%** if there are pictures in the message and you want them to appear full-sized on the printout.
	Choose **Preview in color** if you wish to see an onscreen preview of your print job in color before you print.
Print Range	To print a range of pages instead of all the pages in a document, enter the page numbers in the **From Page** and **To** fields.
Number of Copies	Enter the number of copies of the message you want to print. Choose the collate option when printing multiple copies so your printed documents will be sorted into sets.

After you set your print options, click **OK**, **Preview**, or **Cancel** to finish and close the dialog box.

In this lesson, you learned how to navigate through mail, sort mail, delete mail, set print options, print mail and views, and use folders. In the next lesson, you learn how to create stationery, rules, and out of office notices.

Lesson 5
Using Mail Tools

In this lesson, you learn how to choose letterhead, create stationery, use bookmarks, and activate an Out of Office Message. You also learn how to send a phone message.

Choosing Letterhead

You can select a graphic to appear beside your name in your mail template, and Lotus Notes has several from which to choose.

To select a letterhead, open your mail inbox and choose **Tools, Preferences** on the Action bar. The Preferences dialog box opens. Click on the **Letterhead** tab as shown in Figure 5.1. A list of available letterheads appears in the list box. As you move your cursor over the choices, the graphics appear in the Preview pane. When you find the letterhead you want, click **OK**.

Creating Stationery

Stationery differs from letterhead in that letterhead simply provides a graphic in your mail memo, whereas stationery can contain a graphic, list of recipients, and information in the body of the mail memo. Use stationery for reports that you generate frequently, such as a customer status report. Use stationery when you want to create a signature or use a graphic for a signature. You can create as many different stationery designs as you like. Stationery is stored in your Stationery view and you can create mail memos using stationery at any time.

There are two kinds of stationery you can create: *Memo* stationery and *Personal* stationery. The Memo stationery uses the Mail Memo template, the same template you use when you create an email in Notes.

This template contains only one rich text field—the body field—and has no header or footer fields.

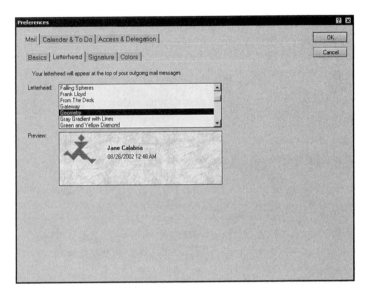

FIGURE 5.1

The Geometry letterhead is selected in the letterhead box and displays in the Preview pane next to your name, just as it will appear in your Lotus Notes mail memo.

Most stationery is based on the Personal Stationery template, as are the instructions in this lesson. Different from Memo Stationery, the Personal Stationery template has a total of three rich text fields to support graphics and formatting at the top and the bottom of the document. The Memo Stationery has only one rich text field.

Because the Memo stationery uses the Mail Memo template, a quick way to create stationery is to create a memo as you would any mail message, by clicking the **New Memo** button on the Action bar. When you have completed the fields you'd like to save, choose **Tools, Save as Stationery**, from the Action bar. This saves your memo as Memo Stationery.

To create Personal stationery, do the following:

1. Open your mail database and click **Tools** in the Navigator Pane, then select **Stationery**.

2. Click the **New** button on the Action bar and choose **Stationery-Personal**.

3. The blank stationery form appears. If you have previously selected a letterhead, the letterhead graphic also appears. If you intend to put your own graphics or photos in your stationery, consider switching back to Plain Text letterhead as shown in Figure 5.2.

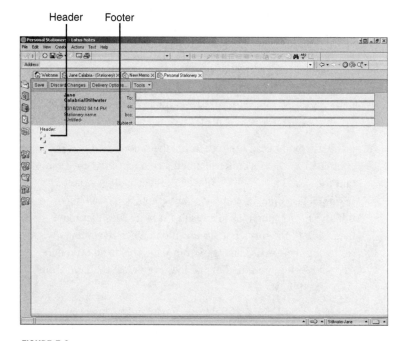

FIGURE 5.2

Blank stationery, ready for your customization. Whenever you create a mail memo using your saved stationery, all fields in the stationery form open in edit mode, allowing you to make changes to this form "on-the-fly."

4. Fill in the header information—the To, cc, bcc, and Subject lines—if you want them to remain the same each time you use this stationery. These important fields are part of the purpose of creating stationery. Information you put into these fields is saved with the form.

5. Fill in the first rich text field that appears in the body of the memo. This is an optional step; however, if you leave this field blank, it appears as a blank field at the time you create a memo using your stationery. In other words, you can't make this field disappear from the form by leaving it blank. Include any graphics or formatted text. This field name (Header) is misleading, since the *header* area of the memo is the area that you completed in the previous step (number 4). Unfortunately, we think Lotus made a bad call when they named this field Header. The result is that this stationery has two headers: one is the header *area*, the other the header *field*, and they are not at all related. To insert graphics in this field, choose **Create, Picture** from the menu and select a graphic from your personal files on your PC.

6. Fill in the body field (optional). It's the second rich text field contained on this form. Remember, a rich text field can contain formatted text (bold, italics, colors) as well as graphics. It's not a good idea to put too many graphics in your stationery form, though, as this results in large files that may take a long time for people to download when they are retrieving their mail messages from you. This is an optional step, but leaving the field blank does not delete the field from your saved form.

7. Fill in the third rich text field: the footer field. This is an optional step but leaving the field blank does not delete the field from your saved form.

8. Click the **Save** button on the Action bar.

9. A dialog box appears, as shown in Figure 5.3. Enter a name for the stationery in the What Would You Like to Call This Stationery? box, and then click **OK**.

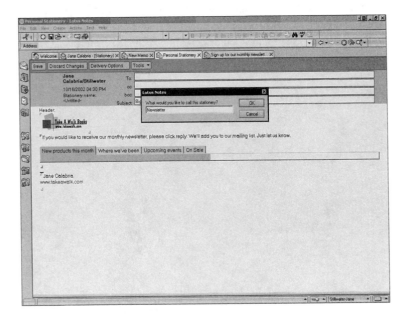

FIGURE 5.3
This Personal stationery contains information that will be used again and again. Each time a monthly newsletter is created. When saving your stationery, create a descriptive and meaningful name so you can easily identify the correct stationery to use in the future.

Figure 5.3 is an example of a Personal Stationery template with a graphic heading and a table in the body field. With this kind of design leverage, you can use your stationery for many reports, such as weekly expense or sales reports.

The stationery is stored in the Stationery folder (see Figure 5.4).

To use your new stationery, go to the Inbox, Drafts, Sent, or All Documents view and click the **Tools** button on the Action bar. Select **New Memo—Using Stationery**. The Select Stationery dialog box appears (see Figure 5.5). Select the stationery template you want to use and then choose **OK**. A new mail message appears, including the elements you incorporated into your template. All fields are in edit mode, so you can make changes to the fields at this time. Note that your changes will not be saved as changes to the form itself; they are only reflected in the memo you are creating. Enter your information and send it as you send any other mail message.

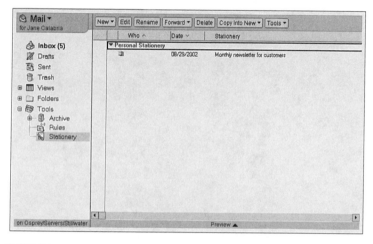

FIGURE 5.4
The Stationery view is the only view that shows a list of stationery you have created and saved. You don't need to be in this view to create new memos with your stationery.

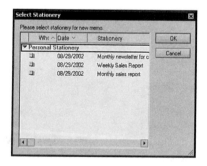

FIGURE 5.5
Choose the stationery for your new memo from the Select Stationery dialog box.

To change your stationery design, select it from the Stationery view and click the **Edit** button on the Action bar. Make your changes and save the document. To delete a stationery, select it in your Stationery folder and press the **Delete** key.

To create *Memo* stationery, follow the preceding instructions for creating Personal stationery, but choose **Memo Stationery** from the **New Stationery** button on the Action bar.

WORKING WITH RULES

Rules determine how Notes handles your incoming mail. You create a rule by defining an action that Notes should take upon receiving email addressed to you. Creating rules is a two-step process: First you create the rule and then you activate the rule. Notes acts on any incoming mail that meets the conditions of the rule you create. If conditions are met, Notes then takes the action you define. For example, you can create a rule that tells Notes that when a memo arrives that has the subject "National Convention," it should move the memo immediately upon receipt into your "Convention" folder. Folders display a number next to the folder icon that indicates the number of unread messages contained in the folder. Because of this new feature of Notes 6, you can quickly tell when new messages have been moved to a folder.

Use the following steps to create a new rule:

1. Open your mail database, open the Tools view, and then open the Rules view.

2. Click the **New Rule** button on the Action bar. The New Rule dialog box appears (see Figure 5.6).

3. Under Create Condition, select the elements of the rule's condition: From the first drop-down list, select the item to look at (sender, subject, importance, To, cc, and so on). From the second drop-down list, select the condition "contains," "does not contain," "is," or "is not". In the third box, type or select the value for which you are looking.

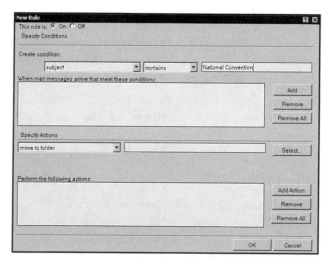

FIGURE 5.6

The New Rule dialog box. When conditions you set are met, Notes takes the action you indicate. If you use rules to move incoming mail into folders, you must remember to check those folders regularly for new mail.

4. Click **Add**.

5. (Optional) To create other conditions for the rule, select **Condition** and then choose **AND** or **OR**—AND to match both conditions, OR to match either. Then enter the second condition. Click **Add**.

6. (Optional) To create a condition under which the rule doesn't apply, select **Exception**. Select or enter the appropriate conditions. Then click **Add**.

7. Under Specify Actions, define what action to take when a memo meets the conditions you set. Click the first drop-down list to select an action such as Move to folder or delete. If you want to move or copy the memo to a folder, click **Select** to open the folders dialog box where you select a folder, and then choose **OK** (you can also create a new folder). Click **Add Action**.

8. After your conditions, exceptions, and actions are defined, click **OK**.

The Rules view lists rules in order of precedence. To position your new rule where it belongs in the list, select it and then click the **Move Up** or **Move Down** button on the Action bar.

To make changes to the rule, select it in the Rules folder and then click **Edit** on the Action bar. The New Rule dialog box opens again so that you can change your settings. Make your modifications to the conditions or actions and then choose OK.

If the rule is getting in the way of your mail management or if you are missing an element that you need when the rule runs, turn the rule off before opening it to edit. To turn rules off or on, click on the rule in the Rules view and click the Disable or Enable button on the Action bar. A rule is enabled when a green check mark shows next to its name.

USING OUT OF OFFICE NOTICES

The Out of Office notice automatically responds to incoming mail messages while you are away from the office. This is a good tool to use when you are away from the office for long periods of time without access to your mail. Prior to your vacation or absence, create a standard message that is automatically sent as a response to incoming messages, notifying others that you are away. You can even create a unique response message to individuals or groups so that some people receive one type of response and others receive a different response.

Use the following steps to create an Out of Office message:

1. Open your mail database. Click the **Tools** button and choose **Out of Office** from the menu.

2. The Out of Office dialog box appears. There are four tabs on this dialog box. On the **Dates** tab, add the dates for **Leaving** and **Returning**. Figure 5.7 shows those fields.

FIGURE 5.7
Out of Office dialog box with Leaving and Returning dates. The Book Busytime option is selected by default. Leave the check in the box so others will see that you are not available when they are searching for free time on your calendar. You learn about free time in Lessons 7, 9, and 10.

3. The Out of Office Message tab provides a place for you to type the Out of Office message (see Figure 5.8) that will be delivered to all people except those who you will list on the Special Message and Exceptions pages. Note that this message will actually be delivered to all people unless you indicate otherwise.

4. (Optional) The **Special Message** tab enables you to provide a message for a special person or a group of people. To select people for this group, click the down arrow button next to the **To** box. When the dialog box appears, select people from your address book, and type your message, as shown in Figure 5.9.

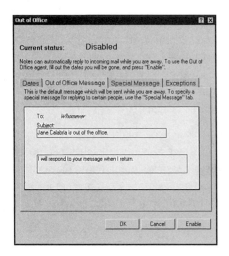

FIGURE 5.8

The customizable basic message is sent as a reply to most emails you receive while you're away.

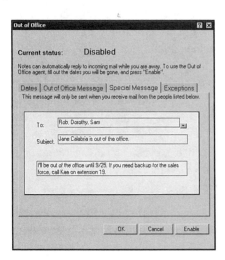

FIGURE 5.9

Select the names of those you'd like to receive a special message. Notes supplies the dates for your out of office message and places them just before your special message so you don't need to include dates in the text of your message.

5. On the **Exceptions** tab, indicate the people and groups who are not to receive any notification in the **Do not automatically reply to mail from these people or groups** field. Click the drop-down arrow key and select people or groups, type the names directly into the field, or leave the field blank if you have no such exceptions.

6. While you're away, you might also get mail that is addressed to a group of which you are a member, and you won't want Out of Offices responses going out to the senders. In this case, enter the names of those groups in the **Do not automatically reply to mail which is addressed to these groups** field.

7. You may be a member of an automatic mailing, in which you don't want Out of Office messages sent. Examples are notices of company meetings, or agents that search databases and notify you with automatic emails. In these cases, you might not know who will be sending the notices, and therefore you can't include them in your exclusions list. However, you can exclude notification by using words or phrases. In the **Do not automatically reply if the subject contains these phrases** field, enter words or phrases (such as *meetings*) you want Notes to look for in the subject line of incoming messages. Note that this applies only to words in the subject line of incoming messages, and that these terms are case sensitive, so you want to enter both *meetings* and *Meetings*. Note too that this does not apply to Internet mailings; for those go to step 8.

8. Consider selecting the **Do not automatically reply to Internet addresses** field only if you have automatic mail sent to you from Web sites, list groups, and so forth and you do not regularly receive mail from others via the Internet. If you regularly receive Internet mail, you'll want to leave this field deselected. (See Figure 5.10.)

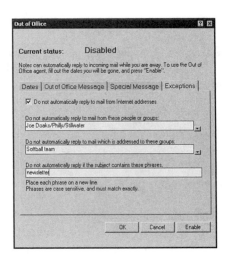

FIGURE 5.10
Enter or select people or groups who are not to receive Out of Office notices.

9. Click the **Enable/Disable** button. A dialog box confirms that the agent is enabled. Click the **OK** button. If you receive a message indicating that you should contact a developer or administrator because you are not allowed to run agents, contact your Notes Administrator for assistance.

If you return to the office on the date that you indicated in the Out of Office dialog box, you don't need to disable Out of Office; it will automatically disable itself. If you return before that date, disable the message using the following steps:

1. Open your inbox. Choose **Tools, Out of Office** from the menu.

2. When the Out of Office dialog box appears, click the **Enable/Disable** button.

DON'T FORGET TO REPLICATE!

If you are a remote user and you have created an Out Of Office message from your remote PC, be certain to replicate your Mail database before leaving for your trip. Otherwise, the server is not notified that this Out of Office Agent needs to run. Refer to Lesson 19, "Using Notes Remotely."

CREATING PHONE MESSAGES

Phone messages are simple, straightforward forms that you use to send telephone message information via Notes. Phone messages work in the same manner as mail messages—fill out the form and click the **Send** button on the Action bar, and the message is mailed to the person or persons in the To, cc, and bcc fields. Use the following steps to create a phone message:

1. With your Mail database open, choose **Create**, **Special**, **Phone Message** from the menu. From another database, choose **Create**, **Mail**, **Special**, **Phone Message**.

2. The Phone Message form appears, as shown in Figure 5.11. Fill in the To field and any other information that you want to supply with this message.

3. Use the rich text field, **Message**, to type any additional information that the caller supplied with his message.

4. Click the **Send** button on the Action bar to send the message.

In this lesson, you learned how to create and customize stationery. You also learned how to create, enable, and disable an Out of Office message and how to create a phone message. In the next lesson, you will learn how to work with Notes utilities and use the Lotus Notes About and Using Documents as well as the Help database.

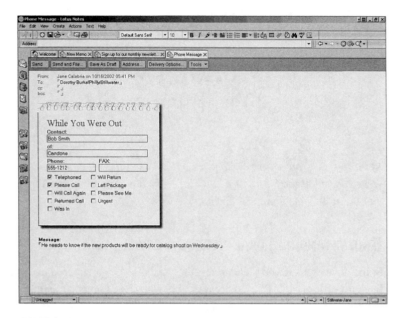

FIGURE 5.11

Add message text to the Phone Message form or simply check the boxes and add the phone number if necessary.

Lesson 6
Working with Databases

In this lesson, you learn how to open a database other than mail, use views, and read the Status bar. You also learn how to access the About *and* Using this Database *documents.*

Understanding Local Versus Server

Some databases are *local* databases; the database files are stored on the hard disk of your PC and are available whenever you need them, regardless of whether you are connected to the Domino server. When you make your changes, additions, and deletions in a local database, no one else sees those changes.

Other databases are stored on the Domino server. This enables you and others in your organization to access information centrally and share it. When you are working on a server database, the changes you make are immediately seen by anyone else who is also accessing that database.

If you are a mobile user, which means your computer is not connected to the server at all times, the local databases you have might be *replicas* of databases on the server. A replica is a specialized form of copy that maintains a link back to the original on the server. When you make changes to your local replica of the database, you are working on your computer with a database that is saved on your hard disk. However, at some point the changes you make to the database are transmitted to the server, and the modifications to the server version of the database are transmitted back to your replica. This process is called *replication*. When you replicate, your computer and the server only exchange the modified or new database documents—not the entire database file. See Lesson 19, "Using Notes Remotely," to learn more about replication.

READING THE ABOUT AND USING DOCUMENTS

Even though your mail database is where you'll spend a lot of time in Notes, Lotus Notes is much more than email. The primary purpose and function of Notes is as a groupware tool—a place for you and your co-workers to come together for discussions, sharing, and editing of documents and information, as well as communication through email. The features and functions of Lotus Notes that you learn in this lesson are common to all databases. The mail and help databases are used for our examples, but what you learn here will apply to any other Lotus Notes databases including those created and provided by your company.

Every database contains two documents to convey to you the purpose of the database and how to use the database. Those documents are the *About this Database* document and the *Using this Database* document. When you open a database for the very first time, the *About this Database* document usually displays.

To view these documents, you must first open a database. To open a database other than mail from a bookmark, click on the Databases button on the Bookmark bar to display the Databases bookmark page (see Figure 6.1). Click **Browse for a Database** to open a database.

Because it's impossible for us to know your company's databases and databases that are available or accessible to you, we're using the mail database as the example in Figure 6.2. To see the *About* document for a database that you have opened (such as mail), choose **Help, About this Database** from the menu. Figure 6.2 shows the *About this Database* document for a mail database. To close the document, press the **Esc** key.

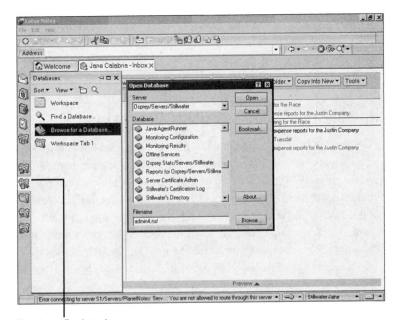

Database Bookmark

FIGURE 6.1
Select a database from your PC (local) or from your server. If you don't have the proper access (rights) to open a database, Notes will notify you.

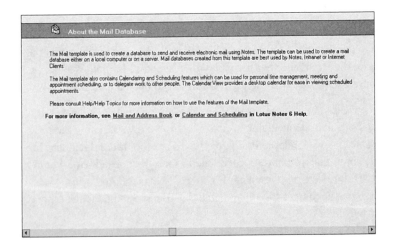

FIGURE 6.2
The About this Database document conveys the purpose of a database.

A database can also contain a Using this Database document. The Using document provides more detailed information on how to use the database. To access the Using document, open a database or select it on the bookmark page and select **Help, Using this Database** from the menu. To close this document, press the **Esc** key. Figure 6.3 shows the *Using this Database* document for a mail database.

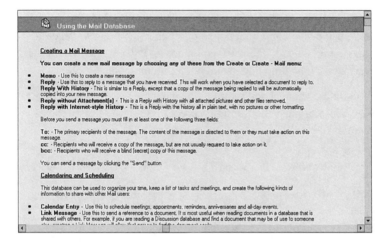

FIGURE 6.3
The Using this Database document provides information on how to use a database.

WORKING WITH VIEWS

When you open a database, Notes displays the contents of the database in a list, called a view. Each line in the database represents one document. Databases often contain more than one view or more than one way of listing information. Some views can be sorted.

Figure 6.4 shows a list of views and folders that are available in the Notes Mail database. From the Mail database, you can send, receive, forward, delete, read, and answer messages. To move from view to view, click the view name in the navigation pane on the left of the mail database workspace.

Often, you can expand or collapse views. A green triangle next to the view name (called a *twistie*) or a "+" or "-" sign indicates that you can expand or collapse the view.

A triangle next to the column title indicates that you can sort the view. In Figure 6.4, you can sort the Who column in ascending order and the Date column in descending order.

To open a document, double-click the document in the view pane. To preview a document without opening it, open the preview pane by dragging up toward the view (see Figure 6.4). Adjust the size of the preview pane by dragging its top border up or down.

To close a document and return to the database list of views, choose **File, Close** or press the **Esc** key. Repeat these steps to close the database.

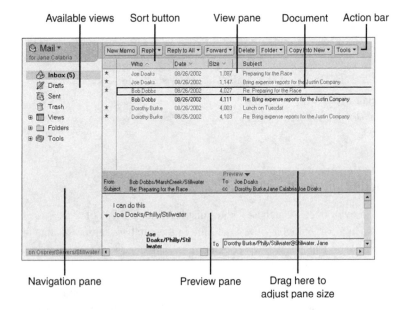

FIGURE 6.4
A view lists the documents of a database; many databases contain more than one view.

READING THE STATUS BAR

The Status bar, located at the bottom of the Notes window, displays messages, icons, and other information you use as you work in Notes. The Status bar is divided into sections; some of these sections display messages, and others lead to a pop-up box or pop-up menu. When a pop-up menu appears, you can select from the menu to make changes in your document or location. Figure 6.5 shows the Status bar.

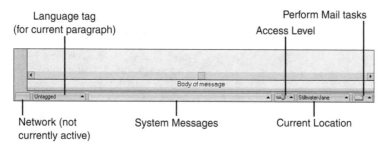

FIGURE 6.5
Use the Status bar for shortcuts and information.

The Status bar is context-sensitive, and the available features depend on the task you are currently performing and the area of Notes in which you are working. Throughout this book, we refer to available options on the Status bar when they apply to the task you are performing. As you can see in Figure 6.5, each section of the Status bar is a button with a specific function. Table 6.1 describes the Status bar buttons and their functions.

TABLE 6.1   Status Bar Buttons

Button	Description
Network	Displays a lightning bolt while Notes is accessing the network; otherwise, the button label is blank. Absence of the lightning bolt does not mean you are not connected to the server. The bolt displays only when the server and your workstation are actively talking to each other.
Language	Displays a pop-up list of languages, with the currently selected language highlighted.
System Messages	Displays system messages about Notes activities. This box is never labeled and is always active. Clicking the messages section displays the last nineteen system messages.
Access Level	Displays a dialog box that shows your status—or level of access—to a database. Clicking the access level displays the level of access you have, as well as the groups and roles that are defined for the database.
Location	Displays your current location. Click the button to see a pop-up menu with choices to change your location.
Perform mail tasks	Displays a pop-up menu from which you can choose Mail options without having to open the Mail database first.

You can modify the Status bar, adding or removing items and establishing the order in which the Status bar items display. To modify the Status bar, choose **File**, **Preferences**, **Status Bar Preferences** from the menu. The Status Bar Preferences dialog box appears as shown in Figure 6.6. Choose the items you want to display on your Status bar by clicking the check boxes. To remove an item, deselect it.

FIGURE 6.6
To change the size of a selected item on the Status bar, use the arrow keys next to the Width preference. You can also change the height, or use the Move Up and Move Down buttons to reorder items on the status bar.

ADDING A DATABASE TO YOUR BOOKMARKS

Opening any database that you have opened before is a simple matter of clicking its bookmark. But what do you do if you want to open a database for which you don't have a bookmark? In that case you must use the menu commands:

1. Choose **File**, **Database**, **Open** from the menu.

2. In the Open Database dialog box, specify the computer on which the database is stored by selecting **Local** or the name of a server from the Server drop-down list.

3. From the Database list box, select the name of the database. If you don't see the name of the database on the list, click **Browse** and locate the database file.

4. If you aren't sure which database you need, click **About** to see the About this Database document.

5. To open the database, click **Open**. The database opens to the About this Database document. Press **Esc** to continue. After you've opened the database, point to the task button and drag it to a bookmark page to create a bookmark for the database. Click on the bookmark page to release it.

6. To add a bookmark for the selected database, click **Bookmark**. When you choose Bookmark, the dialog box stays open so that you can select other databases and add them to your bookmarks. Click **Cancel** to close the dialog box. The new bookmark shows up on the Databases bookmark page.

DELETING DATABASES

Here's the first rule in deleting databases: Don't try to delete databases on the server. In most cases, you wouldn't have the authority to do so. Deleting databases on the server is usually the province of the system administrator. If you want a database removed from the server, contact your system administrator.

Deleting a database is not the same thing as removing the database bookmark from your bookmark pages. If you want to remove a database from your bookmarks, right-click on the database icon and choose **Remove Bookmark**. When you do this, the database disappears from your list of bookmarks. However, the database file still exists on your computer or on the server.

Deleting databases on your own computer is entirely within your control. If you truly want to get rid of a database file on your hard disk, select the bookmark and choose **File**, **Database**, **Delete**. When the warning appears that the action can't be undone, click OK.

In this lesson you learned how to open and close a database. You also learned how to read the *About* and *Using this Database* documents, as well as how to read the Status bar. In the next lesson, you learn how to search and index databases.

LESSON 7
Searching and Indexing Databases

In this lesson you learn how to index a database and how to search a database. You also learn how to search using conditions and how to display and save search results.

INDEX A DATABASE

For Notes to find information within a database, that database must be indexed. The Notes Administrator usually indexes any databases on the server except for your Mail, and then the server updates each index nightly. You won't be able to index databases unless you have Manager or Designer access to the database.

For any local databases or your mail database, you are responsible for the indexing. You create a full-text index only once per database, and Notes takes care of updating the index thereafter.

How do you know when a database has a full-text index or when you need to create one? One way is to check the Database properties box. View the Database properties box for an open database by choosing **File**, **Database**, **Properties** from the menu. For a database that's not open, right-click the bookmark, and choose **Database**, **Properties** from the shortcut menu.

Select the **Full Text** tab in the Database properties box (that's the one with the magnifying glass on the tab). If the database needs to be indexed, "Database is not full text indexed" appears at the top of the Full Text page (see Figure 7.1).

FIGURE 7.1
There is no question that this database needs to be indexed. You can create an index if you have Manager or Designer access. Otherwise, contact your Notes Administrator and ask him to create a full-text index.

Another way to see that a database isn't indexed is to open the Search bar for the database. Choose any database view, and select **View, Search This View** from the menu. The Search bar appears above the View Pane (see Figure 7.2). It indicates whether the database has been indexed. You'll learn more about the Search bar later in this lesson.

To create a full-text index for a database, follow these steps:

1. From the Full Text page of the Database Properties box, click **Create Index**. From the Search bar in a database, click **More**, and then choose **Create Index**.

2. The Create Full-Text Index dialog box appears (see Figure 7.3). Select the options you want to apply to this index.

   Index Attached Files—Select this to be able to search all documents, including the attachments. Select **Without using conversion filters** for a faster, but less comprehensive search (it searches just the ASCII text of the attachments). Choose **Using conversion filters on supported files** for a slower but more comprehensive search.

   Index Encrypted Fields—With this selected, Notes searches all words in fields, including the encrypted fields.

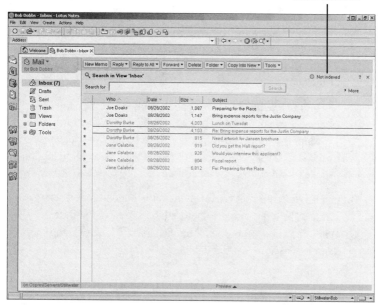

FIGURE 7.2
The Search bar tells you if the Mail database is indexed. "Not Indexed" displays when you need to create an index as shown here.

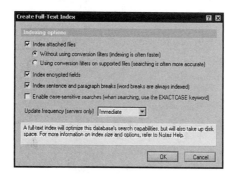

FIGURE 7.3
Be aware that each option you select increases the size of the index and therefore the overall size of the database. However, each additional option you select increases the accuracy of your searches.

Index Sentence and Paragraph Breaks—Select to be able to search for words in the same sentence or paragraph.

Enable Case-Sensitive Searches—Selecting this option means that Notes differentiates between words based on the capitalization (case), so if you're searching for *Home*, the results won't include *HOME* or *home*.

Update Frequency—This option applies to server copies of databases, not to databases on workstations. Your Notes Administrator actually controls this schedule for databases on the server, but you must choose the default **Immediate** option to index local copies of databases.

3. Click **OK**. Your request for indexing is queued to the server. It may take a few minutes before Notes creates the index. When indexing is complete, the Database Properties and the Search bar show that the database is indexed.

SEARCH A DATABASE

The best way to search a database is to search from a view. Open a database view and click the **Search** icon to display the Search bar. Enter the text you want to search for in the Search For text box (commonly called the "search box") and then click **Search**.

The results of the search display in the View Pane (see Figure 7.4). The documents are listed in order of relevance (the gray line in the left margin is darker at the top to indicate greater relevance).

TIP

The Search icon has a drop-down menu, which allows you to search a database, do a Domain search, find people (search an address book), find a database, or open Internet search engines, such as Excite, Lycos, or Yahoo!

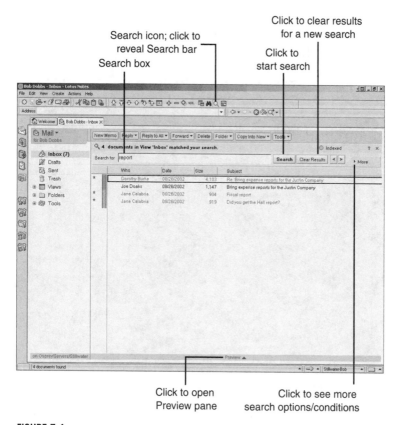

FIGURE 7.4
The most relevant document (the one that exactly matches your search, or the document that contains the most occurrences of your search words) is at the top of the list. It has the search text in both the company name and the contact name.

The Search icon is context sensitive. You can search from a view or from a document while in read or edit mode. When you click the search icon with a document in read or edit mode, a dialog box appears to help you search for text within that document.

When you open one of the documents listed in the search results, every instance of the searched-for text is highlighted in the document (see Figure 7.5).

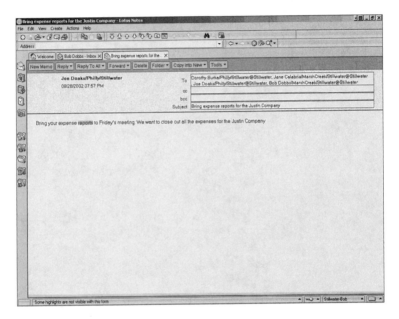

FIGURE 7.5
Searching from a view, the search text was "report," so every occurrence of "report" is highlighted in the resulting documents when opened from that view.

To close the Search bar and your search results, click the **Close** button (×) on the Search bar or click the Search icon. To clear your search and return to your original view, or to keep the Search bar open, click the **Clear Results** button on the Search bar.

QUICK SEARCH

You might not even have to engage the Search bar if the view you're searching is categorized or the first column is set in alphabetical order. Just type a letter or word,

and click **OK**. Notes searches the first column in the
view and stops at the first instance of that letter or
word. Using Quick Search, Notes does not search fields
in the documents other than those that show in the first
column of the view.

SET SEARCH CONDITIONS AND OPTIONS

It's easy to be too specific or too general when searching for information, and in that case, you won't get the results you need. If you're too
general, you may get too many documents returned in your view,
making it difficult to sift through. Using search conditions and options
will refine your search.

USE OPTIONS

There are three options to chose from when searching. The first is
Word Variants, which expands the search to include variations from
the root word (when searching for "bowl" it also looks for "bowling,"
"bowls," "bowler," and so on). The second is **Fuzzy Search**, which
allows some room for misspellings (such as when you type
"Philadlphia," but it still finds "Philadelphia"). The third is **Search
within Results**, which allows you to filter down within a search
you've already run.

To activate these options when the Search bar is open, click **More**.
The Search bar expands (see Figure 7.6). Select **Use Word Variants**
or **Fuzzy Search** or both. Enter the text you are searching for in the
Search box and click **Search**.

USE CONDITIONS

A condition sets criteria that must be met for a document to "match"
the search. You use conditions in combination with your search text.

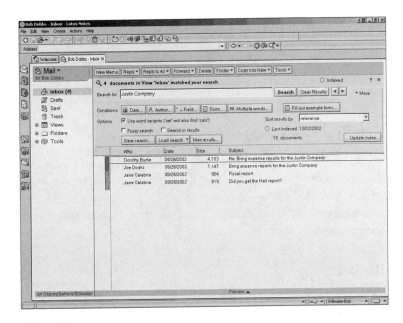

FIGURE 7.6
When you expand the Search bar, you see not only the Options, but the Condition buttons.

With the Search bar displayed, click **More** to expand the Search bar. Click the appropriate condition button to set the criteria for the search. Table 7.1 lists the buttons and describes what they do. When the condition is set, click **Search**.

TABLE 7.1   Search Condition Buttons

Button	Limits Search To	Instructions
Date	Documents that were created or modified in relation to a specific date or time period	Choose **Date Created** or **Date Modified** from the Search for Documents Whose field. Select how the date is to be related to the datevalue (is on, is before, and so on). Specify the number of days or date. Click **OK**.

TABLE 7.1   (continued)

Button	Limits Search To	Instructions
Author	Documents that were created or modified (or not) by the specified author(s)	Choose **Contains** or **Does Not Contain** in the Search For Documents Whose Author field. Then, type in user names (separate names with commas), or click the Author icon and select one or more names from the Names dialog box. Click **OK**.
Field	Documents that contain a specified value in a particular field	Select the field from the Search For Documents Whose field. Choose how you want to evaluate the field from the list (contains, is on, is equal to, and so on). Specify the value for which you are searching. Click **OK**.
Form	Documents that were created using one of the forms in the list box.	From Condition, select **By Form**. Select the form (by form used) from the list. Click **OK**.
Multiple Words	Documents that contain or don't contain specified words or phrases.	In Search For, choose whether to search for the words or phrases you list. Then, in the text boxes, enter the words or phrases for which you want to search. Click **OK**.
Fill out Example Form	The documents that contain specified values in the fields of your example form.	Select the form to use as an example and then fill in the fields where your search words would appear. Notes searches all the forms in your database. To limit the search to only documents created with a specific form, add a "by Form" condition, specifying that example form.

The condition appears next to the search text (see Figure 7.7). It's possible to use more than one condition, although you should try searching using one condition first before further refining the search.

Condition token

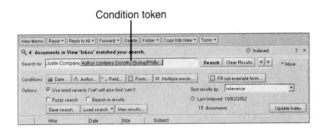

FIGURE 7.7
A condition token appears next to your search text after you define the condition. Double-click the token to open a dialog box and edit the condition. To delete the token, click it once, and then press Delete.

REFINE SEARCHES WITH OPERATORS

An *operator* is a word or character that you type in the Search box to further define the search. For example, typing AND between two words in the search box means you want to find documents where both words appear. Table 7.2 lists popular operators and their variations available for you to use. For a full list of operators, search the Notes Help database for *search operators*.

TABLE 7.2   Search Operators

Operators and Variations	Description
And AND &	Finds documents that contain all the words or conditions combined with the operator. Example: Man AND Woman
* (asterisk)	A wildcard that represents any extension of letters, more than one character per asterisk (doesn't work with dates or numbers). Example: *ow, ho*, *ho*

TABLE 7.2   (continued)

Operators and Variations	Description
CONTAINS Contains = (equal sign)	Specifies that the field before the operator must contain the text that follows the operator. Example: [title] = Favorite. Surround your field names with square brackets.
EXACTCASE Exactcase	Finds documents that contain words where the case matches exactly the example in the Search box. The database's case-sensitive option must be selected. Example: EXACTCASE Notes
Field FIELD [*fieldname*]	Finds documents in which the specified field contains the specified value, using the syntax *FIELD fieldname CONTAINS value*. Example: FIELD LName CONTAINS Dobbs
NOT Not !	Makes query negative. Examples: Man AND NOT Woman, Not [LName] CONTAINS Dobbs, FIELD LName CONTAINS NOT Dobbs
PARAGRAPH Paragraph	Finds documents in which the words around PARAGRAPH are in the same paragraph and then ranks the documents by how close the words are. The database's indexing option must be on. Example: desk PARAGRAPH computer
Or OR | ACCRUE , (comma)	Finds documents that contain either of the conditions or words in combination with the operator. ACCRUE works a little better when sorting results by relevance. Example: Man OR Mouse
? (question mark)	A wildcard that represents any extension of letters—one question mark per character (doesn't work with dates or numbers). Example: ?ow, ho??
" " (quotes)	Place quotes around *and, or, contains,* and so on to have those words treated as words and not as operators.

TABLE 7.2   (continued)

Operators and Variations	Description
SENTENCE Sentence	Finds documents in which the words around SENTENCE are in the same sentence and then ranks the documents by how close the words are. The database's indexing option must be on. Example: desk SENTENCE computer
TERMWEIGHT Termweight	Gives weight to words in document when documents containing the words are found. Use any value between 0 and 65537, with higher number being most important in ranking. Example: TERMWEIGHT 50 manual OR TERMWEIGHT 75 automatic
= (equal to) < (less than) > (greater than) <= (less than or equal to) >= (greater than or equal to)	Numeric operators for use in searching for numbers or dates in number or date fields. Example: FIELD CreateDate > 1/1/1999

DISPLAY SEARCH RESULTS

Unless you dictate otherwise, search results display in order of relevance. To sort the resulting documents in a different order, click **More** on the Search bar. From Sort Results By, select the option you want to use:

- **Relevance**—Sorts the resulting documents according to the number of matches in the document, with the document having the highest number appearing at the top of the list.

- **Last Modified**—Sorts the resulting documents by the date modified, with the latest being at the top of the list.

- **First Modified**—Sorts the resulting documents by the date modified, with the earliest being at the top of the list.

- **Keep Current Order (sortable)**—Leaves the documents in the order they appear in the view (only available if the current view provides column sorting).

- **Show All Documents (sortable)**—Displays all documents in the current view but marks the results as selected (can be sorted if column sorting is active in view).

Too many documents displayed in the results? Limit the number of resulting documents displayed by clicking **Maximum Results**, entering the number of documents you want to see as search results, and then clicking **OK**.

SAVE AND LOAD SEARCHES

If you perform the same search frequently, you can save the search criteria, so you don't need to enter all the conditions and options each time you search.

To save the search criteria, enter any necessary text in the Search box, select the options you need, set the conditions, and specify the display option you want. Then, click **Save Search**. Give the search a name (see Figure 7.8), and then click **OK**.

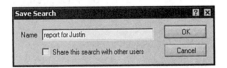

FIGURE 7.8
Enter a name to use when you want to call up this search criteria again.

Later, when you want to use the search you created, you click **More** in the Search bar and then choose **Load Search**. Choose the name from the drop-down menu, and click **Search**.

SAVE YOUR SEARCH RESULTS

If you have access privileges in the database to create a private folder, create one to hold your search results. Choose **Edit**, **Select All** to select all the documents that resulted from the search. Copy the documents into your folder. If you drag the selected documents into your new folder, Notes moves them into the folder and they will no longer appear in your Inbox, so be sure to copy, not move.

Perform a Domain Search

A domain search enables you to search an entire Notes domain for documents, files, and attachments that match your search criteria. You cannot perform a domain search unless the Domino Administrator has set up a server for domain searching and you have access to the domain catalog database where information on all the databases is stored.

To perform a simple domain search, follow these steps:

1. Click the down arrow next to the Search icon.

2. Choose **Domain Search**. The Domain Search form appears (see Figure 7.9).

3. Specify what you are searching for:

   Documents—Searches the titles and content of all Notes documents that are indexed. Click **More** and click the file system check box to search the file system.

   Databases—Searches only database titles listed in the catalog (returns a list of databases).

4. Enter the text you are seeking in the Search box (as you would when searching a view).

Click this button to browse the databases listed in the catalog

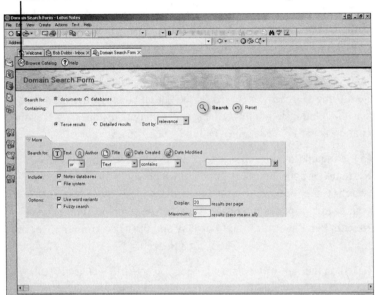

FIGURE 7.9
When you click More, you see buttons and fields that help you refine your search by setting conditions and options. In this example, we further refined our search by selecting Text after clicking More.

5. Select the type of results you want to receive:

> **Terse**—Displays only the relevance, the type (document or file system), the date of the document or file, and the title of the document or URL of the file.

> **Detailed**—Displays the title of the database and the author of the document in addition to all the information included with terse results. If searching the file system, Detailed also displays quite a bit of the document when the document is found in the file system.

6. From the Sort By drop-down list, choose how you want the results sorted: by relevance, by oldest, or by newest.

7. Click **Search**.

To perform a detailed search, follow Steps 1 through 6 in the preceding list. Then, click **More** to display more options. The **Text**, **Author**, **Title**, **Date Created**, and **Date Modified** buttons help refine the search for these specific items. Use any or all of these buttons. For each button you select, a new condition line appears. Each condition line contains a logical operator (and, or, not, and so on), the type of item being searched for (based on the button you selected), text that sets the relationship to the value specified (contains, does not contain, is after, is before, and so on), and the value you enter.

In the Include section, choose to include **Notes Databases**, **File Systems**, or both. Enter categories to which you want to limit your search. Under options, determine whether to **Use Word Variants** in your search or perform a **Fuzzy Search**. You also specify how many **Results Per Page** you want to display and the **Maximum** number of results you want to show. Then, click **Search**.

Based on the type of results and order you specified, Notes lists as many entries as it can find. Only the number of results you specified is displayed on each page (when you search for databases instead of documents, all the results are returned on one page). A description of the number of results represented on the page as a portion of the total shows at the top of each result page. A repeat of what the query was appears on the next line. Previous and Next buttons also appear at the top and bottom of the page to enable you to go back or forward through the pages. To open one of the document or file system entries, click the link at the left of the entry. If the entries are for databases, click the database link icon to open the database.

In this lesson you learned how to index and search databases. In the next lesson you learn how to set mail and calendar preferences.

LESSON 8
Setting Mail and Calendar Preferences

In this lesson, you learn how to set your preferences for your mail database and your calendar.

SPECIFYING MAIL PREFERENCES

Mail preferences determine how your mail works—who can read your mail, whether mail should be encrypted automatically, whether all your outgoing mail is signed by you, and so on.

Complete the following steps to set your mail preferences:

1. Open your mail database.

2. Click the **Tools** button on the Action bar and choose **Preferences**. The Preferences dialog box appears (see Figure 8.1). When the Mail page is active (the default), four tabbed pages appear below Mail: Basics, Letterhead, Signature, and Colors.

3. Click the **Basics** tab, if it's not already displayed. The **This mail file belongs to** field displays your name. To have Notes automatically check the spelling of your mail messages, enable **Automatic Spell Checking**.

4. Click the **Letterhead** tab. Select the default letterhead of your choice. A preview is provided at the bottom of the screen. When you change letterhead, memos created with your previous choice of letterhead do not change. New memos you create after selecting a letterhead here use the new letterhead. You can change letterhead as often as you like.

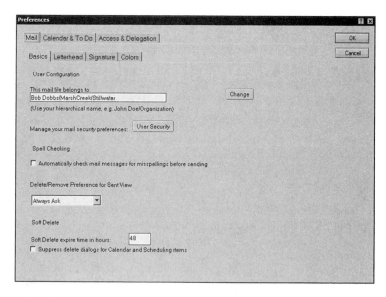

FIGURE 8.1
The Preferences dialog box is divided into three sections—Mail, Calendar, and Access and Delegation—which display as tabs on the first row of the Preferences box.

5. Click the **Signature** tab. Select **Automatically append a signature to the bottom of my outgoing mail messages** if you want your signature added to all your mail memos. A signature can be a piece of text or an HTML file. Don't confuse this signature with electronic signatures, which are an authentication feature as described in Appendix A. To create a text signature, choose **Text** and enter the signature text in the **Signature** box. To use an existing file as your signature, select **File** and enter the name of the file (or click **Browse** and select the file).

6. Click **OK**.

TIP

> Signatures that you create as text cannot be formatted, because the Signature feature of Notes does not allow that. However, if you attach an HTML file, formatting is preserved. If you want a scripted signature, create a signature in your word processing program and format it to your liking. Save it as an HTML file and attach it in the Signature file box.

PLAIN ENGLISH

> **HTML**
>
> Hypertext Markup Language is the coding used to format documents used on the Web.

SETTING CALENDAR PREFERENCES

As you did with your mail, you set up how you want to use the features of the calendar using the calendar preferences. You learn more about using the calendar in the next lesson, but you can set calendar preferences even if you aren't yet familiar with the use of the calendar. For example, in the calendar preferences you set up your free time schedule and determine who can see your schedule. The default free time is Monday through Friday, 9AM to 12PM and then 1PM through 5PM. If your regular work schedule is different than those hours or your lunch hour is different, you'll want your calendar to reflect that. You also specify when and how you want to be reminded of upcoming calendar events, set defaults for calendar entries, choose how time intervals display on your calendar, decide how to process meeting invitations, and specify who can view or manage your calendar.

Complete the following steps to set your calendar preferences (if you did not close the Preferences dialog box after choosing your mail preferences, skip to step 3):

1. Open your mail database.

2. Click the **Tools** button on the Action bar and choose **Preferences**.

3. Click the **Calendar & To Do** tab.

4. Click the **Basics** tabto set the defaults for the calendar. From the drop-down list, select the type of calendar entry you want to automatically appear when you create a new calendar entry. Set the default length for appointments (in minutes) and meetings by specifying the number of minutes in the second box. In the Anniversaries box, enter the number of years for which you want an anniversary to be entered on your calendar. Finally, if you want to enter any personal categories for use in the calendar, type the category text in the **Personal Categories** text box.

5. Click the **Display** tab. To set the length of day you want to see in the calendar pages, indicate when you want the calendar day to start by selecting a time in the **Beginning of the work day** field. Do the same for the ending time in the **at end of the work day** field. Select a number of minutes from the **Each time slot lasts** drop-down list to decide how far apart the times on your calendar should display, as in 60-minute increments, 30-minute increments, and so forth. Choose the **Days displayed in a workweek** by clicking in the box next to the days in the list. You can also choose to start your month view with the current week by selecting the **Start monthly view with current week** field. If you don't want meetings to appear in the All Documents view of Mail select the **Don't display new calendar entries and notices in the All Documents view of Mail**. If you don't want meeting invitations to appear in your Sent View of mail, select **Don't display new meeting invitations in the Sent view of Mail**. If you would like to have your meeting invitations removed from your Inbox after you respond to them, select **Remove meeting invitations from your Inbox after you have responded to them**.

6. Click the **Scheduling** tab (see Figure 8.2), if it's not already displayed. Check the days you want to include in your free time schedule (the time you are available for meetings). Enter the hours of each day you check in which you are available for meetings. (Optional) If you want Notes to check for conflicts when you schedule or accept a meeting, select the option **When adding appointments, accepting meetings, scheduling a meeting.**

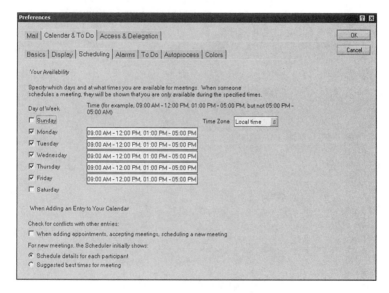

FIGURE 8.2
The Preferences dialog box with the Calendar Scheduling tab selected. Here you indicate which days and times should be considered your default free time.

7. Click the **Alarms** tab. Select **Enable the display of alarm notifications** if you want Notes to alert you of upcoming events that you have entered in your calendar. When you select this field, the dialog box shows new fields, and a list of calendar entry types. Select the types of calendar entries about which you want to be reminded. Then enter the number of minutes or days in advance you want to receive the

reminder. If you want to be alerted by a sound, select the
Default Sound from the drop-down list (if your computer
has sound capabilities).

8. Choose how you want your calendar items to display in your
   mail database under **Displaying Calendar Entries in Mail
   Views**. To display To Do items in a list to the left of your calendar, select **Put C&S documents into a special MiniView
   for processing.** Using this option, the next time you open
   your calendar, the mini view opens as show in Figure 8.3.

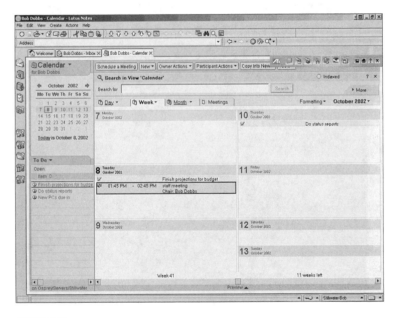

FIGURE 8.3
*The mini view of C&S is selected and all current To Do items appear in the To
Do list. As you take action on the To Do items, they disappear from the list.*

9. To determine how Calendar and To Do items are viewed in
   your mail database, choose from the options shown in Table
   8.1.

TABLE 8.1   Options for Displaying Calendar and To Do items in Your Mail Database

To Do This...	Select This...
To hide calendars entries in your all documents view of mail	Select **Don't display new calendar entries and notices in the All documents view of Mail**
To hide meeting invitations from your sent view of Mail	Select **Don't display new Meeting invitations in the Sent view of Mail**
To hide meeting invitations from your inbox once you have responded to them	Select **Remove meeting invitations from your Inbox after you have responded to them**
To choose which meeting notices should display in your inbox	Select **All** for all Calendar and To Do notices, including invitees' responses to them
	Select **All except responses** to display all Calendar and To Do notices, excluding invitee responses. (If you choose this option, when you want to see responses, look in your All Documents view in Mail, View Invitee Status per meeting, or look in your Meetings view in Calendar.)
	Select **None** to hide all Calendar and To Do entries from your Inbox.

10. Click the **Autoprocess** tab to determine how you want to process meeting requests. You must manually respond to all requests for meetings unless you choose **Enable automatic responses to meeting invitations**. By choosing this, Notes will automatically respond to meeting invitations that arrive in your Inbox. Once you choose this option, you must then select from the following:

When a meeting invitation is received from—Anyone is a default setting for this field, but you can use the drop-down menu to select a list of people, or a list of exceptions.

You must also tell Notes what actions to take when meeting invitations arrive: if you choose **Automatically accept if time is available**, Notes will automatically accept any meeting invitations for you if the time of the proposed meeting is free in your free time schedule. If you're busy at the time of the proposed meeting, Notes auto-declines the meeting, but places a memo in your Inbox titled "Declined Meeting Name" so you can accept later. If you choose **Automatically decline if time is not available**, Notes will automatically decline meeting invitations that conflict with free time shown on your calendar. When you choose **Let me decide if time is not available**, Notes will give you the option of attending or not, regardless of your schedule.

You can also delegate meeting invitations to another person. In the **Perform the following actions** drop-down field, select **Delegate invitations to the following person instead of me.** By choosing this option, Notes forwards all meeting invitations to the person you specify (the person you enter in the Delegee field). This is useful if someone else manages your calendar. The person who invited you to the meeting will receive notice that you have appointed a delegee to this meeting.

11. Two options are available in the Automatic Inbox Management section: The first is **Prompt to confirm deletion**, which results in Notes prompting you when you delete a calendar notice from your Inbox or any view in your Mail Database. The second, **Remove from this view/folder with prompting**, results in no prompting by Notes when you make such deletions.

12. Click the To Do tab. Select **Do not display To Do entries in the calendar** if you don't want your To Do list to display in your calendar. You will still see To Do's in your To Do view. Select **Allow Notes to update To Do status and dates for incomplete entries** if you want incomplete To Do's to show on the current date of your calendar.

13. Click the **Colors** tab to choose your color preferences for calendar items.

14. Click **OK**.

SETTING ACCESS & DELEGATION PREFERENCES

The Access & Delegation preferences are divided into three tabbed pages: Access to your Mail and Calendar, Access to your Schedule, and Shortcuts to Others' Mail. On these pages, you determine who can access your mail (see Figure 8.4), who can access your free time, who can see your calendar entries, who can create calendar entries in your calendar, and so forth. If you make no changes and accept the program defaults, no one can access your mail, everyone has access to your free time (but they can't see the details or names of entries in your calendar), and you have no shortcuts to access the mail databases of other people.

To set Access and Delegation preferences, follow these steps (if the Preferences box is open, skip to step 3:

1. Open your mail database.

2. Click the **Tools** button on the Action bar and choose **Preferences**.

3. Click the **Access and Delegation** tab (see Figure 8.4). On the **Access to your Mail and Calendar** page, click **Add Person or Group** and select the person or group you want to permit access to your mail or calendar entries (see Figure 8.5).

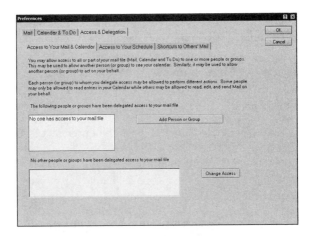

FIGURE 8.4
The default setting for accessing your mail is no one. When you add someone to the access list, you'll have the opportunity to designate their level of access.

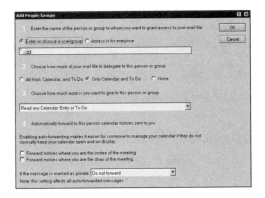

FIGURE 8.5
In Step 1 you add a person or group to your access list. In Step 2, you add the level of access you want to give, and the options in Step 3 change depending upon the level of access you select in Step 2.

In Step 2, choose how much of your mail file you want to grant access to. See Table 8.2 for an explanation of access levels.

In Step 3, choose the level of access you want to give for your mail, calendar, and To Do items. See Table 8.2 for a detailed explanation of level of access. The choices in the drop-down section of Step 3 change according to the choices you made in Step 2.

In Step 4, if you want Notes to automatically forward notices to the person listed in Step 1, choose either **Forward notices where you are the invitee** (when you receive meeting invitations they will automatically be forwarded to the person listed in Step 1), or **Forward notices where you are the Chair of the meeting** (when you receive calendar notices where you are the Chairperson, they will be automatically forwarded to the person listed in Step 1).

If in #2, You Chose...	Select This Option	For This Level of Access
All Mail, Calendar and To Do	Read Any Document	Allows the person or group you designate to read your email (but not encrypted mail), calendar entries (but not details of entries marked private), and To Do items (but not those you mark private).
	Read and Create any Document, Send Mail on your Behalf.	The same as the preceding selection, but they can also send mail from your database. When they send mail from your database, the mail is identified to the recipients as a memo created by the delegee, and sent on your behalf (By Jane Calabria on behalf of Dorothy Burke).
	Read, edit, and create, and send mail on your behalf.	Same as previous, but also allows the delegee to edit your mail.

If in #2, You Chose...	Select This Option	For This Level of Access
	Read, edit, create, and delete any document, send mail on your behalf.	Same as previous but also allows the delegee to delete any document in your mail database.
	Read and create any document, delete any document they created.	Restricts the delegee to deleting only those documents they created in your database.
Only calendar and To Do	Read any Calendar Entry or To Do	Allows delegee to read your Calendar and To Do items; not your email and calendar items you marked as *private*.
	Read, create, edit and delete any Calendar Entry or To Do	Same as previous but also allows delegee to edit and delete Calendar and To Do items.
None	No options offered	

Allowing others to see your schedule information is different than allowing them to see your calendar entries. By default, when others are scheduling a meeting and they check your availability; that is, they have access to see that your time is free or not free. There are two sections to the scheduling page: First, **Who is allowed to see your schedule information (when you are busy or available)** is where you give access to individuals or groups to your scheduling information. The default is **Everyone may see your schedule information**. To make changes to the default, choose **No one** or select an individual or group from the drop-down list. The second section is **What schedule information they may see** and the default here is **Only information about when you are busy or available**. You can choose **Detailed information about your calendar entries** if you want everyone to see appointments on your calendar when they are looking for your available time, or choose

Only information about when you are busy or available, except the following people may see detailed information and in the drop-down menu, select the people that you want to see your calendar entries.

CAUTION

You do not have to give out your password for others to access your mail or calendar information if you grant them access through the Preferences dialog box. Never give out your password. When you give people access to your mail database, they can't read your encrypted mail sent to you, and you can't read encrypted messages they create on your behalf unless your User ID contains the encryption key used to encrypt the messages. Consult with your Administrator if you need to read each other's encrypted mail or if your designee needs to send encrypted mail on your behalf.

OPENING SOMEONE'S MAIL, CALENDAR, AND TO DO

For others to read mail, send mail, set appointments, and use the rights you have just given them, they need to open your mail database, or if you've been given rights to others' databases, you need to open their mail database. The easiest way to access the calendar and mail to which you have rights is to add a shortcut. To do so, open your mail inbox, and choose **Tools, Preferences**. On the **Access and Delegation** page, choose **Shortcut to others' mail**. Use the drop-down menu to choose people from the address book who have given you access to their mail or calendars (see Figure 8.6).

USING THE NOTES MINDER

As long as you have your Notes client running, even minimized, you receive notification of any new mail. If you exit Notes, however, you have no idea that a new, and possibly urgent, memo has been delivered to your Mail database.

FIGURE 8.6
Right-click next to Mail and you'll see the shortcuts you created to access the mail and calendars of others.

Notes has a utility that notifies you of new mail and any Calendar alarms, even when you aren't running your Notes client. The utility is called the *Notes Minder*. When Notes Minder is running, an envelope icon displays in the system tray of your Windows 95/Windows 98/Windows NT/Windows 2000/Windows XP taskbar. The current status or number of new mail messages received pops up when your mouse point points to the icon. For example, it might read "Mail last checked at 4:45 PM." Double-clicking the icon launches Notes in your Mail file.

Start Notes Minder initially by choosing **Programs, Lotus Applications, Notes Minder** from the Start menu (click Start on the Windows taskbar). Your Notes client does not have to be open.

Alternately, have the utility automatically start when you log on to your computer by putting the executable file in the Start folder. To do this in Windows 98, Windows 2000, or Windows XP, choose **Settings, Taskbar & Start Menu** from the Start menu. Click the **Start Menu Programs** tab, and then choose **Add**. Click **Browse**, and locate the Notes Minder executable file (nminder.exe in the Notes folder). Select it, and choose **Open**. Click **Next**, and then double-click the **StartUp** folder in the **Select Folder to Place Shortcut In** list. Click **Finish**. To do this in Windows 95 or NT 4.0, check the Help files of these operating systems under "start up."

Clicking on the Notes Minder icon with the right mouse button pops up a menu (see Figure 8.7).

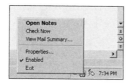

FIGURE 8.7
Right-clicking the Notes Minder icon displays a pop-up menu.

Select a menu choice to do one of the following:

- **Open Notes** opens the Notes client and displays your Inbox.

- **Check Now** checks the status of your Mail file.

- **View Mail Summary** opens a dialog box that displays the unread messages in your Inbox. Double-clicking one of the messages in the Unread Mail Summary dialog box opens the Notes client and displays that message. To close the dialog box without viewing a mail message, click OK.

- **Properties** displays the Options for the Lotus Notes Minder dialog box (see Figure 8.9). In the Properties box, you set the types of notifications you want to receive (audible, visual, and/or missed alarms). You also specify how frequently you want the Notes Minder to check for incoming mail, or you can disable checking. Click OK to close the dialog box.

FIGURE 8.8
Specify whether you want to receive audible or visual notification when you get new mail, or both.

- **Enabled** has a check mark when Notes Minder is enabled. You click this menu selection to enable or disable the Notes Minder.

- **Exit** exits the Notes Minder.

In this lesson, you learned how to set your preferences for both mail and the calendar, how to choose letterhead, and how to use Notes Minder. In the next lesson, you learn how to use the calendar.

LESSON 9
Using the Calendar

In this lesson, you learn how to open and select calendar views, make entries in your calendar, check available time of others for meetings, respond to meeting invitations, and print the calendar.

Some Calendar entries affect your free time availability. Managing access to your calendar, who can read it and who can see when you are available, was covered in Lesson 8, "Setting Mail and Calendar Preferences." You might want to revisit that lesson to set your Calendar preferences before using the Calendar.

SELECTING CALENDAR VIEWS

To open your calendar, click the Calendar bookmark or select **Calendar** from the Welcome Page, as shown in Figure 9.1. If your mail database is already opened, you can click the calendar bookmark, as shown in Figure 9.2.

The default views for the Calendar are day, week, month, and meeting. These views are available by clicking on the tabs at the top of your Calendar (see Figure 9.3). Click the triangle next to the Day, Month, or Week to see more choices. For example, available views for Day include one day or two day, and views for Week include a work week or full week.

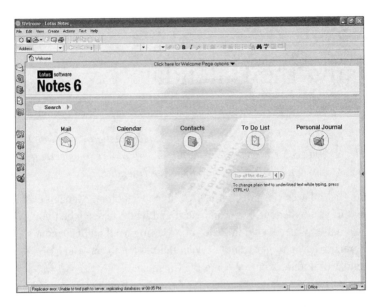

FIGURE 9.1
Access your Calendar from the Welcome Page.

You can quickly go to a different date or change the month or year by using the Date Picker (see Figure 9.4).

You can also view details about calendar entries by using the Preview Pane as shown in Figure 9.5.

UNDERSTANDING CALENDAR ENTRIES

When you create calendar entries, they must fall into one of several categories:

- An **Appointment** is an entry in your calendar that does not include the process of inviting others in Notes. Appointments can have a start and end time, can be set to repeat, and can be marked private so that even those with access to your calendar cannot read the particulars about private appointments.

Calendar icon

FIGURE 9.2
Optionally open the calendar from your Mail database by clicking on the Calendar bookmark.

- An **Anniversary** is an occasion that has no time value, such as a birthday, working holiday, or payday. Anniversaries do not affect your free time. Anniversaries appear on your calendar only and can be set to repeat.

- **All Day Events** have a duration of at least one full day. Unlike appointments and invitations, you cannot specify a start time or end time. Events are typically used to schedule vacations, seminars, conventions, and the like.

- **Reminders** are notes to yourself that display on your Calendar on the time and date you assign to them. Reminders have a beginning time, but no time value (that is, no ending time). They display on your Calendar only, and can be set to repeat. One common use is a reminder to make a phone call. Do not confuse Reminders with Alarms or To Do's.

Click triangle for more view options

Day | Week view | Meetings
Date Picker | view | Month view | view | Action bar

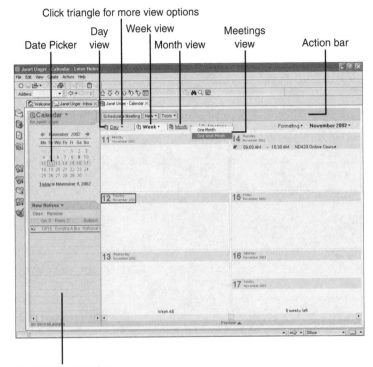

New Notices mini view

FIGURE 9.3
The Calendar tabbed pages contain additional view options. This Calendar also contains the New Notices MiniView.

- **Meeting Invitations** are appointments in which you include and invite others from your organization. If those you invite are part of your Domino Mail system, Meeting Invitations are distributed to the participants' Inboxes. Meetings also appear on the Calendars of invited participants when the participants have accepted the invitation. Like appointments, meetings have time values, have a beginning time and ending time within one calendar day, and can be set to repeat. You can send meeting invitations to people over the Internet and they will receive a text message, but not all of the formatting and graphics you see in the Notes form.

Click here to change days

Click here to change months or years

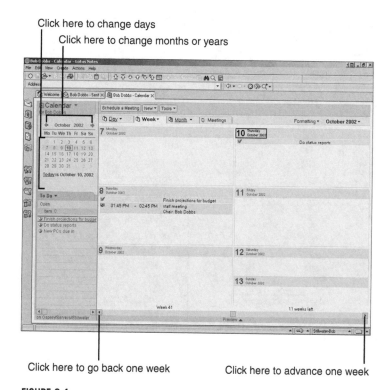

Click here to go back one week   Click here to advance one week

FIGURE 9.4

Change your date quickly and easily with the Date Picker.

CREATING A CALENDAR ENTRY

The steps for creating an appointment, anniversary, reminder, or event
are similar. Here, we discuss creating those kinds of calendar entries.
The steps for scheduling a meeting are found in Lesson 10, "Working
with Meetings and Group Calendaring," under "Scheduling Meetings."

You can create a calendar entry at any time while in Lotus Notes. To
create a calendar entry, do one of the following:

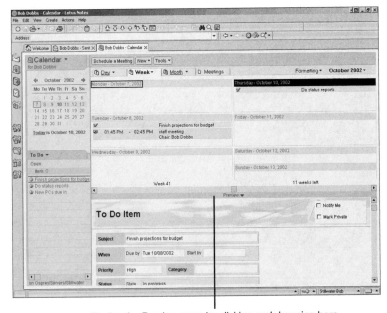

Resize the Preview pane by clicking and dragging here

FIGURE 9.5
Click the Preview Pane triangle to open or close the Preview Pane.

From your Calendar View—To create an **Appointment**, **Anniversary**, **Reminder**, or All Day **Event**, click the **New** button on the Action bar. To create a meeting, click the **Schedule a Meeting** button on the Action bar.

From within the a specific day—Double-click a date or time slot in the Calendar displayed in the Calendar View. Choose the Calendar Entry type from the drop-down list.

From outside of the Calendar—Choose **Create, Calendar Entry** from the menu.

You can change the type of calendar entry after the entry form opens by clicking on the down arrow next to the type (such as Appointment) to open a dialog box that allows you to select another type.

Depending on the type of calendar entry you create, the entry fields vary slightly. Figure 9.6 shows the calendar event form for an appointment.

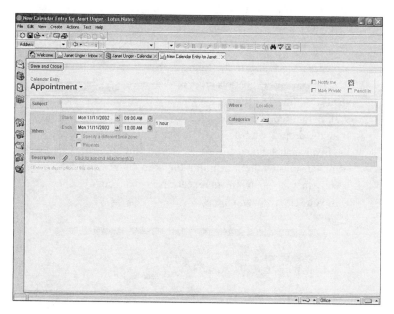

FIGURE 9.6
Appointments have an option field that allows you to add an attachment.

Use your mouse cursor or the **Tab** key to move from field to field when creating a calendar entry. Remember the fields available to you depend upon the type of calendar entry you're making, so you may not see all these fields in an All Day Event or a Reminder.

   Subject—Type in several words that describe the calendar entry. These words will appear in the Calendar View, and if sent to anyone else, in the Subject column in the Inbox.

   When (Starts and Ends)—Type in the start time and end time for the calendar entry. If you click the clock icon, you will see a time scale. Drag the indicators up or down the scale to set the time and duration of the appointment. Use the up and down triangles to see different parts of the scale. Click the green check mark to accept the time setting.

Specify a Different Time Zone—If you specify a different time zone, new fields appear to help you select the time zone. You will also see a Local box that shows what time this will be locally.

Repeats—Place an **x** in the **Repeats** check box to set parameters for calendar entries that occur more than once, such as a weekly status meeting. The Repeat Options dialog box appears (see Figure 9.7). In the Repeat Rules dialog box, select the **Repeat** interval from the drop-down list. Based on that choice, set the specifics of the frequency and intervals. Then, set the **Starting** date. Choose an ending date using the **continuing for** or **to** fields. Click **OK**. If you specify that the appointment repeats, new menu choices appear to help you select repeat options.

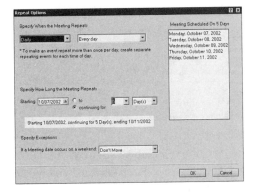

FIGURE 9.7
Fields in the Repeat Options dialog box change, depending on the type of repeat you select (monthly by date, weekly, and so forth).

Description—Use this area to provide a more detailed description of the calendar entry. For example, you might want to supply an agenda for a proposed meeting. The Details field is a rich-text field, allowing you to apply text and paragraph formatting, as well as to insert file attachments and embed objects.

Pencil In—Place an **x** in the check box to have the calendar entry appear on your Calendar, but have others still see this time as available if they check your schedule.

Mark Private—This option is important if you have given other individuals access to *read* your Calendar. Placing an **x** in the check box prevents the other calendar readers from seeing this appointment. Use this if you want to enter a confidential calendar entry such as a doctor's visit. Others will see that your time is blocked, but will not have access to the appointment information.

Notify Me—Place an **x** in the **Notify Me** check box or click the alarm clock icon to set the parameters for seeing and hearing a reminder for this calendar entry. In the Alarm Notification Options dialog box, specify when you want the alarm to go off, the on-screen message, the sound to play, and whether you want an email notification to go to others.

GOOD MORNING!

Imagine yourself at home, snuggled up sleeping in your bed. The ringing of your phone shatters the still of the night. "Hello?" A digitized voice rasps, "This is your Lotus Notes notification. You have a meeting at 10:00 a.m. with the Production Team." *NOT!* Your computer must be on and you must have Lotus Notes open (even if minimized), or you must have Notes Minder running to see or hear calendar entry notifications.

Categorize—Select the category for this calendar entry document from the pull-down list. Personal Categories are defined in your Calendar Preferences (**Tools, Preferences**). Review Lesson 8 for more information about setting Calendar preferences.

COLOR CODING CALENDAR ENTRIES

You can select the background and text colors for the different types
of calendar entries if you are connected to your mail server and your
server is running Lotus Domino 6 server software.

To set colors from the Calendar View, choose **Tools, Preferences** from
the menu. On the Calendar and To Do page, click the Colors tab. For
each color you want to change, click the arrow in the **Background
Color** or **Text Color** fields. Choose your colors from the palette using
the sliders or eyedropper as shown in Figure 9.8. When you are finished selecting your colors, click **OK** to save your choices and close
the dialog box.

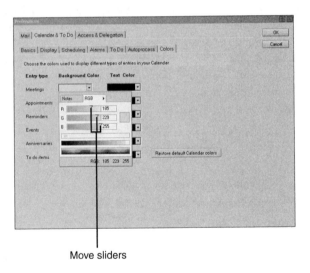

Move sliders

FIGURE 9.8
*Move the sliders to select your color (R=Red, G=Green, B=Blue). If you want to
return to the default Notes Calendar colors, click the Restore default calendar
colors button.*

Customizing the Entries

You can change the way that calendar entries appear in your Calendar. Figure 9.9 shows the default calendar entry display.

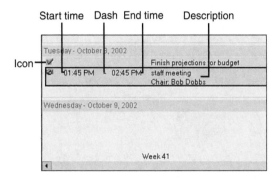

FIGURE 9.9
The standard calendar entry displays an icon, start and end time, and description.

This customized entry shown in Figure 9.10 displays an icon, start time, and description.

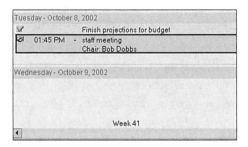

FIGURE 9.10
In this customized view, we've removed the end time for calendar entries.

To customize your Calendar View

1. Open the Calendar and choose **View, Customize this View** from the menu.

2. (Optional) Select or deselect the items you want to display in the Customize View dialog box (see Figure 9.11).

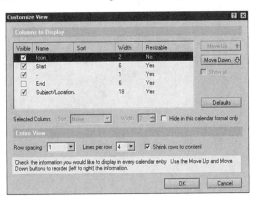

FIGURE 9.11
You can change field width and lines per row for your calendar entry displays in this dialog box.

3. (Optional) Use the Move Up and Move Down buttons to change the order in which items appear in your calendar entry. To return to the default settings, click the Defaults button.

4. (Optional) Choose the Hide in this calendar format only field to have your new selections apply to the current view (week, month, and so forth) of your calendar, but not in other views.

5. (Optional) Change the format for field width, row spacing, and lines per row in the **Entire View** section.

6. Click **OK** to save your changes and close the dialog box.

Printing the Calendar

Notes 6 has many choices for printing Calendars, and those choices
are a great improvement over previous versions of Notes. When you
print your calendar in 6, you can choose to include or exclude week-
ends, you can print banner headings, and you can select from a large
list of formats such as Day-Timer and DayRunner formats.

To print a Calendar View, do the following:

1. Choose **File**, **Print** from the menu.

2. Select your **Printer**, **What to Print** (in this case, your calendar), Print Quality, and Print Range on the Printer Tab (see
   Figure 9.12).

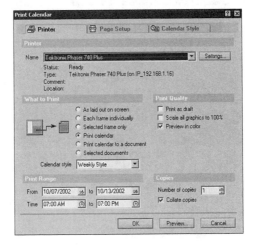

FIGURE 9.12
Your Print Range includes both dates and times for printing your calendar.

3. Click on the Calendar Style page. Under **What to Print in
   Every Calendar Entry**, choose the fields you want to print
   in your Calendar (you can change the order of fields using
   the Up or Down buttons).

4. Under **Style Options**, place a check mark next to those options you wish to select for your calendar print job.

5. Under **Page Types** choose the type of page you wish to print. A Full Page is 8.5×11 paper.

6. To preview your Calendar before printing (we highly recommend this) click the Preview Button (see Figure 9.13).

7. If you need to change the page setup, click the **Page Setup** Tab. Here you can change the size of paper, margins, and so forth. Page setup is beyond the scope of this book; however, you can find directions and information in the Notes Help Database by searching for "page setup."

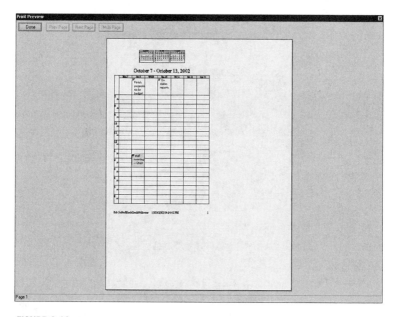

FIGURE 9.13

This preview shows a Calendar with the Franklin Day Planner Classic page type selected. Note that the calendar is off center. This is because Notes assumes I'm using a perforated form, which I can tear and fit into my Franklin Day Planner.

Editing Calendar Entries

Our calendars aren't carved in stone—appointments get rescheduled, events are postponed, and meetings are called off. Notes supports your needs to modify calendar entries, move them to different dates, or delete them.

To modify a calendar entry, double-click the entry in Calendar View to open the document. You can alter any of the fields in the document, including Entry Type, to change the type of Calendar entry for the document. Save and close the document to have your changes take effect.

If you have a repeating entry, such as a weekly appointment, any changes you make to the any of the entries will affect the related repeats. For example, say you try to change the start time for the appointment. The Change Repeating Entry dialog box appears and presents choices for how you want your changes to affect the related entries. You can choose to affect only the entry you have open, all the repeated entries related to this entry, only this and previous repeated entries, or only this and future repeated entries. Make your selection, and then choose **OK**.

You cannot change the days on which a repeating entry occurs, but you can delete future dates and re-enter the entry.

NO REPEATS

You can only set repeating entries when you create a calendar entry. You can't add repeating entries to an existing entry.

Although you can edit a calendar entry and change the dates and times, it's often quicker to drag and drop the appointment to the new date or time. When you drop the appointment in a new slot or day, the Reschedule Options dialog box appears. The new date or time you dragged to appears as the Start and End; click OK to confirm. However, if you drag a meeting entry for which you are not the owner, the Propose Options dialog box appears so you can suggest a different date or time for the meeting; an email is sent to the owner requesting the proposed change of time.

To drag an entry to a time you can't see on a date, hold the entry over one of the scroll arrows on the date and the Reschedule Options dialog box will appear. Needless to say, when you want to drag an entry to a new time, be sure the times show on the screen by clicking Formatting at the top right of the Calendar screen and selecting Show Time Slots.

If Notes asks whether you're sure you want to move the entry, click **Yes**.

When you need to delete a calendar entry, open your Calendar, click the entry to select it (hold down **Shift** and click additional entries to select more than one), and then press **Delete**. Be very sure you want to delete the entry, because you won't be able to get it back.

Converting Calendar Entries

Mail messages you receive might contain information about appointments you need to make, events you need to attend, upcoming dates about which you want to remind yourself, or other date-related information. You can take that information directly from your mail message and convert it into a calendar entry.

Select or open the mail message, and click the **Copy Into New** button on the Action bar. Select **New Calendar Entry**. A new entry document opens (see Figure 9.14). The **Subject** of the new entry matches the Subject line of the mail message. The body of the mail memo is added to the **Description** of the entry, but a horizontal line appears above it along with space for you to add any comments relating to the entry you're creating. From that point, make any changes you need to the entry, and then save it.

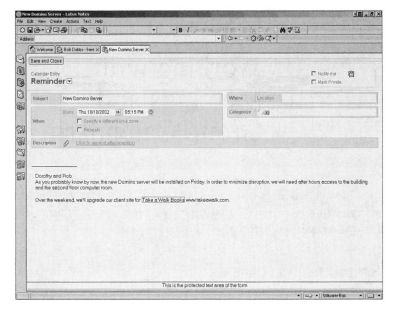

FIGURE 9.14
This reminder entry was based on an email that Bob Dobbs received regarding an upgrade project.

Calendar entries can likewise be used to generate mail memos. Select the entry in the Calendar View and then click **Copy Into New** on the Action bar. Choose **New Memo**. A new mail memo opens, and the Subject of the Calendar entry becomes the subject of the mail memo. You complete the memo and send it to the recipients you specify.

You can also create To Do tasks from selected calendar entries, Click the **Copy Into New** button and choose **New To Do**.

In this lesson, you learned how to switch Calendar Views, create and edit calendar entries, and print Calendars. In the next lesson, you learn how to create meetings and work with Group Calendaring.

Lesson 10

Working with Meetings and Group Calendaring

In this lesson you learn how to schedule and edit meetings, respond to meeting invitations, create Group Calendars, make entries in the Group Calendar, and view other Calendars.

Scheduling Meetings

Lotus Notes is an ideal product for organizing group activities. Notes helps you to schedule meetings and invite participants, as well as to reserve rooms and resources for those meetings. In addition, Notes enables you to create a Calendar for a specific group (or project) that is shared by those you define as the group.

When you identify a need for a meeting, you must inform all the people involved of the meeting time and place—and, of course, that their attendance is requested. Do this by creating a meeting invitation. The first time you create a meeting invitation, it will take you some time to learn to use all the meeting invitation features, including how to view the free time of others. After you create one or two meeting invitations, you'll find that this task is easy and quick. The steps to creating an invitation are the following:

- Create the invitation.

- Identify the invitees and others whom you want to inform about this meeting.

- Check the time of the invitees and (optionally) schedule your meeting time according to their availability.

- Determine how you want your invitees to respond to your meeting.
- Mail the meeting invitation.

To begin, open your Calendar and follow these steps:

1. With your Calendar open, click the **Schedule a Meeting** button on the Action bar.

2. In the Meeting document (see Figure 10.1), enter a brief description for the meeting in the **Subject** field.

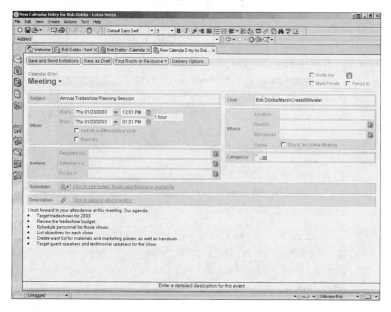

FIGURE 10.1
Enter the general meeting information on the Basics page.

3. Enter or select the **Starts** and **Ends** dates and times (click the button at the right end of the field to see a date or use the Time Picker).

4. For a meeting that will occur at regular intervals (such as a monthly meeting), select **Repeats** and enter your repeat options.

5. For a meeting that will fall within a different time zone, choose **Specify a different time zone** and enter the time zone information.

6. In the **Invitees** field, enter the names of people you want to invite to the meeting (click the button at the right end of the field to select names from an Address Book).

7. (Optional) To provide a copy of the invitation to someone that informs him and keeps him updated about the meeting but doesn't *invite* him to the meeting, enter the person's name in the **cc** or **bcc** field. Use the **bcc** field only if you don't want other recipients to see the name of the person receiving an information-only copy of the invitation.

8. In the **Description** field (see Figure 10.2), enter important facts about your meeting, such as its purpose, directions to the location of the meeting, and so forth. You can embed files in this rich text field, such as supporting data for your meeting, and you can also attach a file by clicking the **Click to append attachment(s)** button.

9. To check the availability of your invitees, click the **Click to see Invitee, Room and Resource availability** button in the **Scheduler** section of the form.

10. Be sure the **Details** radio button is selected in the **Show** section for this exercise. The Free Timesection appears (see Figure 10.3). You can see the free time of each invitee (shown in white) sorted by the names of the invitees, by the week, by who can attend, by who cannot attend, or by whose time wasn't found. If the schedule is okay for everyone—that is, if a green bar appears for all names—go to Step 12.

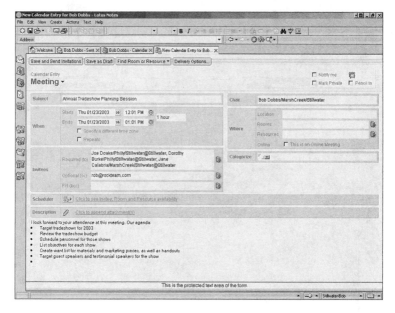

FIGURE 10.2
Enter the names of the invitees in the appropriate Required (To), Optional (CC) and FYI (BCC) fields.

RESTRICTED OR NO INFO SCHEDULES

These people have either changed their Calendar preferences so that others cannot see their free time, or there is a problem with their Calendar and they need to talk with the Notes Administrator.

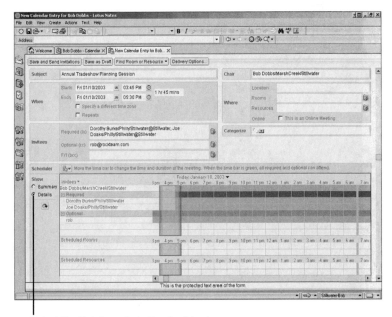

Select the Details radio button for this view

FIGURE 10.3
The details view of the Show field displays available times. A green bar indicates everyone is available; a red bar indicate there is a conflict.

11. If you see a conflict (time shows in red) in the schedule, do one of the following:

   • Select a time from the **Recommended meeting times** field by clicking on the Summary radio button (see Figure 10.4). Double-click a suggested time in the summary, or select it and click the Use Selected Time button.

   • Set a new date or time in the **Date** or **Time** field.

   • Click the **Change Invitee List** button to add or remove people.

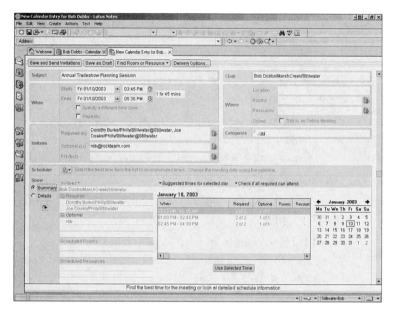

FIGURE 10.4
summary view of the Show field displays suggested available times for all invitees.

12. When the Free Time dialog box indicates that the meeting time is okay (green) for everyone, click the **OK** button to close the box and continue with your meeting invitation. To schedule a resource, continue with step 13; otherwise, go to step 14.

13. (Optional) Click the helper button at the right end of the **Rooms** box to book a room for the meeting. Click the **Resources** helper button to reserve resources, such as audio-visual equipment, for the meeting. Handling these reservations is covered more fully later in this lesson.

14. Check **Pencil In** to keep the time of this meeting available in your free time schedule. Select **Mark Private** to prevent people who have access to your Calendar from reading the invitation. To set up a notification for the upcoming meeting,

click **Notify Me** and pick the appropriate Alarm Options. From the **Categorize** field, select an appropriate category for the meeting.

15. Click the **Delivery Options** button on the Action bar to set any of the following options:

    • Set the **Delivery Report** and **Delivery Priority** as you would set them for email delivery. (Refer to Lesson 3, "Creating and Sending Mail," for more information.)

    • **Return Receipt** Check this box if you want notification that your meeting invitation has been received by the recipient(s).

    • **I Do Not Want to Receive Replies from Participants** sends the invitation as a broadcast message that doesn't require a reply. Use this for large, general meetings where attendance is always required or there is such a large number of people invited that individual responses would be overwhelming.

    • **Prevent Counter-Proposing** stops the recipient from proposing a different time schedule for the meeting.

    • **Prevent Delegating** keeps the recipient from delegating attendance to another individual.

    • **Sign** adds a digital signature to the invitation to guarantee that you are the person who sent it.

    • **Encrypt** encrypts the invitation so only intended recipients can read it.

16. Save the invitation and send it to the invitees by clicking the **Save and Send Invitations** button on the Action bar. Alternately, click **Save as Draft** on the Action bar to save the invitation as a draft and send it at a later time.

Meetings can be held online, too, if your group works with Lotus Sametime. If you check **This is an Online Meeting** in the Where section of the Meeting form, new fields appear. Choose a

Type—Collaboration, Moderated presentation/demo, or Broadcast meeting—and enter the URL for the meeting in Place. You can also add meeting attachments, such as whiteboards.

MANAGING MEETINGS

After you have scheduled a meeting, you want to manage the meeting by checking on the status of responses to your meeting, rescheduling meetings when necessary, and possibly sending mail memos that relate to the meeting. All this management of the meeting can be done with the Notes Calendar and Notes Mail.

The Meetings View of your Calendar displays a list of meeting invitations, both the ones you issued and those sent to you (see Figure 10.5). Use this view to quickly locate a meeting and open it. The meetings are listed in date order, oldest at the top.

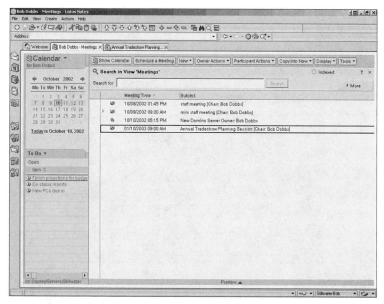

FIGURE 10.5

The Meetings View lists the meetings in date order, oldest to newest, and also shows the responses from the invitees. Click on the Meeting Time heading and you can change the order of appearance.

Using Action buttons in this view, you can create new Meetings, take Owner actions on selected meetings, or take Participant actions on selected meetings. You can also copy meeting information into new memos, calendar entries, and To Do's.

To reschedule a meeting, follow these steps:

1. Open your Calendar and click the Meetings View. Select the meeting you want to change.

2. Click the **Owner Actions** button on the Action bar, and select **Reschedule**.

3. The Reschedule Options dialog box opens (see Figure 10.6).

4. Modify the **Begins** and **Ends** dates or times (click **Check Schedules** to use the free time schedule to see when your invitees are available).

5. Click **OK**. Notices will be sent to the invitees, informing them of the change of date or time. By checking **Include Additional Comments on Notice** in the dialog box, you can add a short explanation along with the notice.

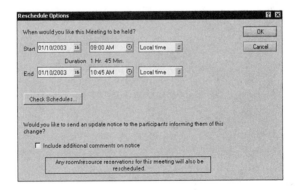

FIGURE 10.6
Room and Resources are automatically rescheduled when you reschedule the meeting.

When you cancel a meeting, you need to notify all the participants that the meeting has been cancelled. The steps for canceling a meeting are as follows:

1. Select the meeting document in the Meetings View of the Calendar.

2. Click the **Owner Actions** button on the Action bar, and select **Cancel**.

3. The Cancel Options dialog box appears (see Figure 10.7).

4. If you selected **Permanently Delete the Meeting and all notices and documents related to the meeting,** Notes removes any documents related to the meeting. Or, you can remove the meeting from your Calendar but leave it in your Meetings View. Again, you have the option to include a message along with the notice. Click **OK** to close the dialog box. Notes automatically sends a cancellation notice to all the invitees for that meeting.

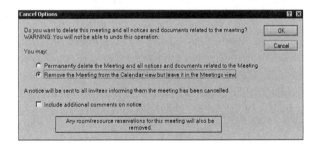

FIGURE 10.7
Notes automatically notifies all invitees of the cancellation and can clean up all related documents.

After you have received the responses to your meeting invitation, you should remove the names of invitees who won't be attending from the meeting document. You should then send a confirmation notice to the remaining invitees to let them know the meeting is indeed on at the

time and date specified. The notice will include the new list of participants for the meeting. To confirm a meeting, follow these steps:

1. Select the document from the Meetings view of the Calendar.

2. Click the **Owner Actions** button on the Action bar, and select
   Confirm.

3. (Optional) Select **Include Additional Comments on Notice**
   in the dialog box to give yourself the chance to add your own
   text to the notice.

4. Click **OK** to close the dialog box.

Although the Meetings View displays response documents to meeting
invitations, it's not easy to determine whether all the invitees have
responded and accepted. To quickly review the status of the responses
to your invitation, follow these steps:

1. Select the meeting in the Meetings View.

2. Click the Actions button on the Action bar and choose
   Owner Actions, and then select **View Invitee Status**.

3. The Invitee Status dialog box opens (see Figure 10.8), displaying the list of invitees, including optional or FYI invitees
   who were copied on the invitation. The dialog box displays
   the role of each person and the status of the invitation.

4. Click **Print** to print the list or **Close** to close the dialog box.

If you want to send a memo to all meeting participants to update the
agenda or to provide more details about the upcoming meeting, follow
these steps:

1. Select the meeting in the Meetings View.

2. Click the **Owner Actions** button on the Action bar, and
   choose **Send Memo to All invitees**, **Send Memo to Invitees
   who have responded**, or **Send memo to Invitees who have
   not responded**.

Click here to expand or collapse

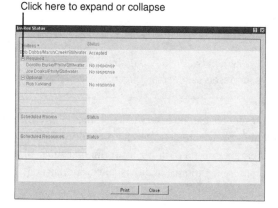

FIGURE 10.8
You expand or collapse the Invitee status information by clicking the plus or minus signs next to the Required or Optional lists.

3. A new mail memo opens. The list of invitees appears in the **To** field, and optional invitees are in the **cc** or **bcc** field (depending on where you listed them in the meeting invitation).

4. The **Subject** field contains only the name of the meeting. The message area is blank, and you can create a message there as you would in any mail memo.

5. Click **Send** to send the memo to the invitees.

MAKING ROOM AND RESOURCE RESERVATIONS

Part of creating the meeting invitation is to specify and reserve a room and any equipment to be used for the meeting. As you learned earlier in this lesson, you can reserve a room or resource from the Meeting Invitations & Reservations page of a meeting invitation while you are creating an invitation, or even after the meeting has been scheduled. You can also reserve a room or resource using the Scheduler button on the Action bar after a meeting has been saved.

TIP

> To reserve rooms and resources, your organization must have rooms or resources in its Directory (Address Book). Check with your Notes Administrator if you don't see such resources in your Directory.

Rooms and resources can be reserved using one of two methods: Reserve them by their names (overhead projector or Ellis Room), or search for them by criteria (conference room that seats 10 people) or categories (conference rooms, audiovisual equipment).

CAUTION

> If you have difficulty or questions regarding room or resource reservations, consult with your Help Desk or your Notes Administrator. Our instructions assume that resources are included in your Directory and that Sites and Categories have been assigned.

To reserve a room or resource by name, follow these steps:

1. Open a meeting invitation.

2. (To reserve a room) In the **Where** section, enter the name of the room you want to use in the **Rooms** field, or click the button at the right end of the field to select from a list of rooms.

3. (To reserve a resource) In the **Where** section, enter the name of the resource in the **Resources** field or select the name from the list that appears when you click the button for that field.

To search for a room by criteria (Site and/or seating capacity), follow these steps:

1. Open the meeting invitation and click the **Find Room or Resource** button on the Action bar.

2. Select a site in the drop-down menu of the **Site:** field. Sites are an optional service set up by the Notes Administrator. If no sites are available, this field can be left blank.

3. Enter the **# of attendees** in that field. The number of attendees helps Notes to find a room based on its seating capacity. Don't leave this field blank.

4. Click the **Search** button.

5. Under **Search Results**, select the room you want to reserve, and click **OK**.

6. When you save the meeting entry, Notes sends a reservation request to your organization's Directory. This room is now "booked" and will not appear as an available resource during the time and date you have booked it.

To search for a resource, follow the preceding steps but choose Find Resource instead of Find Room.

Should you need to cancel a room or reservation (if you don't cancel the entire meeting), open the meeting invitation and click **Remove** next to the Rooms or Resources field. Save the invitation.

RESPONDING TO MEETING INVITATIONS

You can accept or decline an invitation to a meeting. Unless prevented by the sender of the invitation, you can also propose a different meeting time that is more suitable for you, or delegate the meeting to someone else.

ARE YOU FREE?

Don't assume that the owner of the invitation checked your free time before inviting you to the meeting. To be sure you have the time available, click the **Check Calendar** button on the Action bar to see what you have scheduled for the day of the meeting before you respond to the invitation.

When you receive the invitation in your Mail, you open the document. Click the **Respond**, **Respond with Comments**, **Request Information**, or **Check Calendar** button on the Action bar (see Figure 10.9).

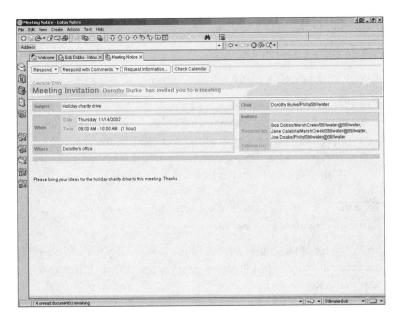

FIGURE 10.9
You can check your Calendar before responding to a meeting invitation by clicking the Check Calendar button.

NO RESPOND BUTTON?

The sender does not expect an answer to the meeting invitation because the memo is a broadcast invitation. Click **Add to Calendar** to add the meeting to your Calendar. Click **Request Information** if you want to know more about the meeting.

Choose one of the following:

- **Accept** accepts the invitation. A memo of acceptance is sent, and an entry for the meeting appears on your Calendar.

- **Decline** rejects the invitation. A memo is sent noting that you decline the invitation.

- **Delegate** declines the invitation for you, but enables you to specify the person to whom you want the invitation sent. Notes then forwards the invitation to that person. This option might not be available if the owner of the invitation chose to prevent delegation.

- **Propose New Time** gives you the opportunity to propose an alternate meeting time that is more convenient for your schedule. You specify the new date or time and click **OK**. A counterproposal memo goes to the invitation sender, but it displays the changes in schedule you propose. That proposal can also be accepted or declined. The Propose New Time option might not be available if the owner of the invitation chose to prevent new time proposals.

- **Tentatively Accept** accepts the meeting invitation, adds the meeting as an entry to your Calendar, but enables the **Pencil in** option on the Options page of the entry so the time still appears as free in your free time schedule.

REPEATS

If the meeting invitation is for a repeating meeting, your answer applies to each instance of the meeting. Check your schedule before you reply. Also, be aware you can't counter-propose for repeat meetings. You must first accept the invitation, then double-click the first instance in your Calendar of the meetings, click **Respond**, and choose **Propose New Time**.

If you chose **Respond with Comments**, add your comments to your answer. Click **Send** to send your response.

Rather than responding individually to each meeting invitation, Notes can automatically answer them for you. Click the **Tools** button on the Action bar in the Calendar. Select **Preferences**. Click the **Calendar & To Do** tab and then the **Autoprocess** tab.

Select **Enable automatic responses to meeting invitations**. Then complete the following fields:

- **When a meeting invitation is received from**—Use the drop-down list to select those people whose meeting invitations you would like to send automatic responses.

- **Perform the following action**—Use the drop-down menu to select **Automatically accept if time is available.** If you make this selection, you must then choose **and automatically decline if time is not available** or **and let me decide if time is not available**.

- Alternately, you can select **Delegate invitation to the following person instead of me**. Then, add the person's name to the **Delegee** field.

- **Automatic Inbox Management**—From the drop-down menu, choose an action for Notes to take when you delete a calendar notice from your Inbox or Mail folder. The choices are **Prompt to confirm deletion** or **Remove from this view/folder without prompting**.

Creating a New Group Calendar

A Group Calendar displays the free time schedules of a specified group of people. You quickly see who in the group is available or busy at a particular time. If you have access to their individual Calendars, you can display them below the Group Calendar.

To open a Group Calendar, open your Calendar and click **Tools, View and create Group Calendars** from the Action bar. The Group Calendars View opens. If you want to create a new Group Calendar, click the **New Group Calendar** button on the Action bar and select the names of those you would like included in your Calendar. The Group Calendar opens as shown in Figure 10.10.

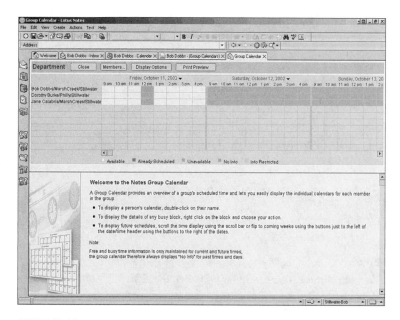

FIGURE 10.10

The Group Calendar displays the free time of all the members of the group. To display the details of any busy block, click it. If you have access to that Calendar, the event will appear at the bottom of the screen; otherwise, you see instructions on how to use the Group Calendar.

OLD DATES?

Group Calendars only display current and future dates. Older dates are marked as "No Info."

You determine the starting time of the Group Calendar and the total number of hours shown for each day. Click the **Display Options** button on the Action bar. In the Options dialog box (see Figure 10.11), select a **Starting Time** and **Duration**. Then, click **OK**.

FIGURE 10.11
In this dialog box, set the total number of hours showing for every day on the Calendar and the time the days begin.

Once you have created Group Calendars, they appear in the group Calendar list. To open one of the Calendars, double-click on its name.

Editing or Deleting a Group Calendar

From the Group Calendars View, any selected Group Calendar can be edited or deleted.

Editing a Group Calendar involves changing the members or the title. You select the Group Calendar and click the **Edit** Action button. The New Group Calendar dialog box appears, so you can add or remove members or modify the title of the Group Calendar. Make your changes, and click **OK**.

To delete a Group Calendar, select it in the Group Calendars folder and then click the **Delete** button on the Action bar. The Group Calendar document disappears but can be seen in the Trash folder in Mail. Permanently remove the Group Calendar when you refresh your view, exit the mail database, or click **Empty Trash** on the Action bar of the Trash folder. Confirm the deletion.

In this lesson you learned how to work with group calendaring and how to schedule, manage, and accept or decline meeting invitations. In the next lesson you learn how to work with To Do items.

LESSON 11
Working with To Do Items

In this lesson, you learn how to create items for your personal To Do list, how to keep track of your personal To Do list, and how to assign tasks to others by creating a To Do task.

CREATING TO DO ITEMS

To help keep track of all the things you have to do, create a personal To Do item. Once created, a To Do item (optionally) displays in your calendar and is also found in your To Do view. To access the To Do view (as shown in Figure 11.1) click the To Do bookmark. You can also switch to your To Do view by clicking on the word **Mail** in the Navigator pane of your mail database and choosing **Switch to To Do** from the drop-down list.

In previous versions of Lotus Notes, To Do items were called *tasks*, and we prefer to use *tasks*, so you might find we use these two terms interchangeably throughout this book.

To create a personal To Do entry, do the following:

1. Open your mail database or your calendar. Click the To Do bookmark on the left of your screen. The To Do view opens, as shown in Figure 11.1.

2. Click the **New To Do Item** button on the Action bar. The New Personal To Do form appears, as shown in Figure 11.2.

3. (**Optional**) Select **Mark Private** if you do not want to give access to this To Do item to others to whom you give access to your email.

To Do bookmark

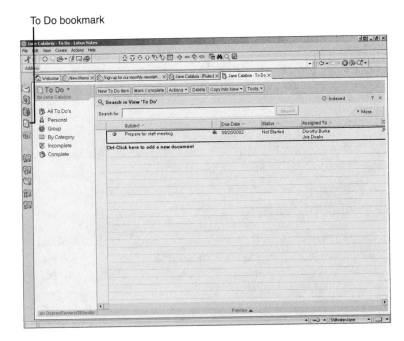

FIGURE 11.1
The To Do view is accessed by clicking the To Do bookmark.

4. Choose to assign this task to yourself or to others. If you select others, the form changes so you can add a list of assignees, as shown in Figure 11.3.

5. Enter a description for this To Do item in the **Subject** field.

6. To establish a start date for the task, enter the date in the **Starts** box or click the **Date** icon next to the box to select a date from the drop-down calendar.

7. (**Optional**) If you have a repetitive task, select **Repeats**. The Repeat Options dialog box appears (see Figure 11.4). Under Repeat, select the frequency of the repeat (such as **Monthly by Day**, then **Every other month on the**, and then the day). Under Continuing, specify when the repeating task ends by

setting a time period or an ending date. To prevent the due
date of the task from falling on a weekend, select an option
under If the Date Occurs on a Weekend. Choose **OK** to close
the dialog box. If you need to go back and change the
Recurrence options later, click the **Settings** button. If you
save a To Do item before you set Repeats, you cannot change
it to a repeating To Do item; you must re-create it from
scratch.

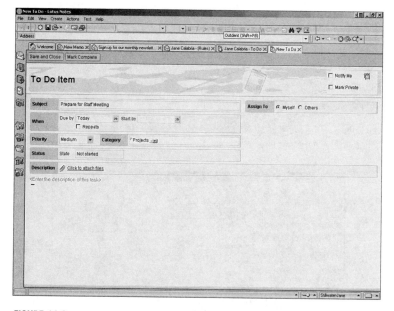

FIGURE 11.2

*The To Do form in Lotus Notes 6 is different and more streamlined than previous
versions.*

8. Enter a date in the **Due** box to set a due date for the task, or
   click the **Date** icon next to the box to select a date from the
   drop-down calendar.

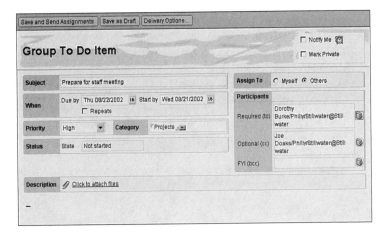

FIGURE 11.3
Complete the participant fields as you would complete the header of an email. The three fields here represent to:, cc:, and bcc: fields of an email. Others will automatically be notified by email when you save this To Do item. By assigning this to others, this becomes a "group to do" item.

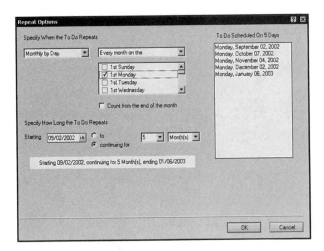

FIGURE 11.4
The Repeat Options dialog box is the same dialog box you see when you create a repeating calendar entry, such as a meeting.

9. **(Optional)** To receive a reminder when the task is due, select **Notify Me**. The Alarm Options dialog box appears. Enter the number of **Minutes, Hours,** or **Days** either **Before** or **After** the due date you want to be alerted. Enter a message to display at that time. If you want a sound alarm, select **Play sound** and choose a sound in the drop-down list. To have a mail message sent, click **Send mail with entry title and description** and select recipients from the drop-down box that appears. When you are finished, choose **OK** to close the dialog box.

10. To set a priority for the task, click **High, Medium, Low,** or **None** (the default is **Medium**). Setting this priority affects the order that To Do items appear in your To Do List. Those with a high priority will appear with an icon labeled "1" and will appear before any 2s (medium priorities) and any 3s (low priorities). All no-priority tasks appear last on their respective dates in your To Do views.

11. **(Optional)** Choose an appropriate Category such as **Holiday** or Vacation from the drop-down list, or type your own category in the **Categorize** field.

12. To attach files to this To Do item, click the Attach Files field and choose a file or files to attach.

13. **(Optional)** If you are assigning this to others, click the **Delivery Options** button on the Action bar to set the following options:

    - Choose your **Delivery Report, Delivery Priority,** and **Return Receipt** options. These options are the same as the options you find when you send a Mail Memo.

    - Check **I do not want to review replies from participants** if you do not require the participants to respond to your assignment.

- Check **Prevent count-proposing** to prevent the recipient from sending the task back to you with a counter proposal.

- Check **Prevent delegating** if you do not want the recipient to assign this task to someone else.

- Check **Sign** and/or **Encrypt** to encrypt or attach an electronic signature to the memo.

14. Click the **Save and Close** button (available if you're making a personal To Do), the **Save and Send Assignments** button (available if you're assigning to others), or the **Save as Draft** button (to save it in your drafts view) on the Action bar to save the task. The task appears in your To Do view.

In addition to displaying in your To Do view, To Do items also appear in your calendar. You can change the default settings of Notes if you do not want To Do items to appear in your calendar. See Lesson 20, "Customizing Notes," for more information.

To edit a To Do item, simply click once in the Subject field and you can edit it while in your To Do view. You can also double-click a To Do item to edit it.

CONVERTING MAIL MESSAGES TO TO DO ITEMS

Convert mail messages to To Do items so that they appear in your To Do list. For example, you can convert a mail message from your manager that asks you to prepare your department's budget for next year to a task, which adds that message to your To Do list so that you won't forget to follow up. To convert a mail message to a task, do the following:

1. Select the document in your Inbox view pane or open the message.

2. Click the **Copy Into New** button on the Action bar. Select **New To Do**.

3. A new Group To Do opens. The subject of the mail message appears as the Subject. The mail message becomes the Details. You can make any changes or additions you want to the information provided there.

4. If you want to assign the task to yourself, click the **Save and Close** button on the Action bar, or press the **Esc** key.

    To assign the task to anyone else, click **Assign to others** and fill in the recipient fields.

You also can create new tasks from Calendar entries. If you're creating an entry that also happens to be the deadline for a task, choose **Copy Into New, New To Do** from the menu. Change any information in the new To Do document and then save and close it.

Existing tasks often generate new tasks, and you can create new tasks from an existing task document. With the existing task selected or open, choose **Actions, Copy Into, New To Do** from the menu. Complete the new To Do document, save it, and close it.

Viewing To Do Status

To keep track of the tasks you assign to yourself, tasks others assign to you, and tasks you assign to others, open the To Do view in the Mail database.

Several views are available for the To Do List: **All To Do's, Personal, Group, By Category, Incomplete**, and **Complete.** You can change the status of an item by completing it and clicking the **Mark Complete** button on the Action bar. You can also cancel or reschedule a group To Do by choosing **Actions, Reschedule** or **Cancel** from the Action bar.

RESPONDING TO A TO DO ITEM

When you are named as a participant on a To Do document, you
receive a mail message in your Inbox. When you open the message,
you find choices for responding to this To Do assignment on the
Action bar. Click the appropriate button on the Action bar:

- **Respond**—Click here to **Accept** or **Decline** the task,
  Delegate the task to another person, or **Propose New Time**,
  which allows you to change the due date. If you delegate the
  task, you must name a person to handle the task. However,
  you can request updates from the owner of the task (the person who created the To Do document). You can also receive
  updates if you decline the task. The last choice in this menu
  is **Completed**, which marks the task as completed and notifies the sender that you have completed the task.

- **Respond with Comments**—Contains the same choices as
  found in the Respond menu, but the return form includes a
  field for you to add comments when accepting, declining,
  delegating, proposing a new time, or completing the item.

- **Request Information**—Click here to ask for further information before or after accepting the task. When you select this,
  you also have the opportunity to **Include comments on the
  reply message**.

When you select a response option, a mail message is generated and
sent to the owner of the task. When the owner receives your response,
he too has options, which are available under the **Actions** button on
the Action bar in the To Do view. These include the following:

- Reschedule

- Cancel

- Confirm

- View Invitee Status

- Send Memo to Invitees who have responded

- Send Memo to Invitees who have not responded

In this lesson, you learned how to assign tasks to yourself and to others, how to mark the tasks as completed, and how to view the tasks. In the next lesson, you will learn how to use the Address Books.

LESSON 12
Using the Address Books

In this lesson, you learn about the two address books found in Lotus Notes—the Public Address Book and the Personal Address Book—and how to use your Personal Address Book for creating Business Cards and Groups.

DEFINING THE ADDRESS BOOKS

Like Notes Mail, Notes Address Books are databases. Email addresses, phone numbers, and other contact information is stored in your Address Book. At least two address books are available to you: Your Personal Address Book and your Company Address Book (sometimes referred to as the Domino Directory, or the Public Address Book; see Figure 12.1) .

Your *Personal Address Book* has your name on it and is empty until you add people to it. In contrast, the Company Address Book, or *Directory*, contains the addresses of employees in your company who use Lotus Notes Mail, and it has your company's name on it. Your Domino system administrator maintains this address book.

USING YOUR PERSONAL ADDRESS BOOK

As is the case with your Mail database, the contents of the Personal Address Book are controlled completely by you and you are the *Manager* (see Appendix A for a complete explanation of security and access rights) of this database. You're the only one who can read, modify, or delete contact entries. You don't need to add your fellow employees, because everyone in your company is already in the

Domino Directory, so avoid duplicating entries that might already be found there. However, remote users (those who use Notes out of the office, at home, or on their laptops) should add people from the Public Address Book to their Personal Address Book because they may need to access the Domino Directory when they're not connected to the Domino server. For more information on remote users, see Lessons 19, "Using Notes Remotely."

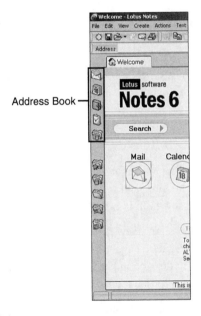

Address Book

FIGURE 12.1
Click the address book icon to access your personal database. To have quick access to a Domino Directory, open the directory on the server by choosing File, Database, Open and bookmark the directory in your Favorites or Database book-marks.

After you click the Address Book bookmark, the Personal Address Book Navigation Pane displays the following views:

- **Contacts**—The people you have in your Personal Address Book are listed with their telephone numbers and company information. (If you are new to Lotus Notes Mail, your address book is probably empty.)

- **Contacts By Category**—The same people that are listed in your Contacts view, but now they are sorted into categories that you create.

- **Groups**—Lists the groups of people you created as mailing distribution lists.

- **Birthdays and Anniversaries**—Lists the dates of birthdays and anniversaries of contacts. Of course, if you don't include a birthday or anniversary date of a contact in their contact information, they won't show in this view. Don't confuse this with anniversary dates you create in your calendar.

CREATING CONTACTS

The information you store about a person—name, title, company, address, phone, fax, email address, and so on—is kept in a Contact document, such as the one shown in Figure 12.2.

To create a Contact document for a new person, click the **New Contact** hotspot on your Welcome Page, or open your Address Book and click the **New** button on the Action bar and choose **Contact**. The following describes the fields for adding a new contact.

- At the top level of this form are fields for names, title, suffix, and email. The last name field is a required field unless you also fill in the company field in the Business section. In other words, you can have a contact named Joe if you provide Joe's company. Or you can have a contact named Joe Doaks with no company name. But you cannot save a contact whose only information is a first name.

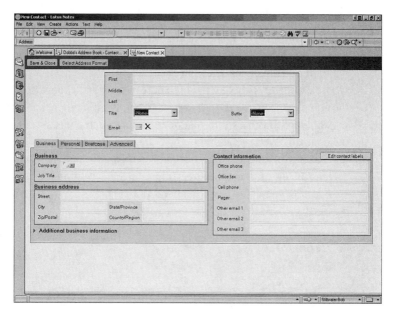

FIGURE 12.2
Tabs separate the sections of a Contact document, and you can keep business as well as personal contact information.

- When you fill in the **Email** address field, be sure to click the icon on the left of the field. Here, you'll tell Notes what kind of email client you're adding. This information helps Notes to format the text in your email behind the scenes and helps ensure that text formatting you choose in Notes gets reformatted so that a non-Notes user can read your formatted text. If you don't know the details then don't make a selection, but if, at the very least, you know enough about the contact to choose Notes or Internet, choose one of those two. If you have more than one email address for a contact, type the email address you use most for them in the email field and put the remaining email addresses in the Other Email fields on the bottom left of the Business tab section.

- The **Business** section of the contact contains, appropriately, business information about that contact such as their company name, job title, and so forth. Click the drop-down arrow button if you are creating a contact document for a person whose company is already in your address book and choose the company from the drop-down list. Click the triangle next to Additional Business Information to include such items as the company Web site address. There are no required fields here, so if you only know part of the business information such as the city, but not the street address, you can fill in the information you know (see Figure 12.3).

Click here...

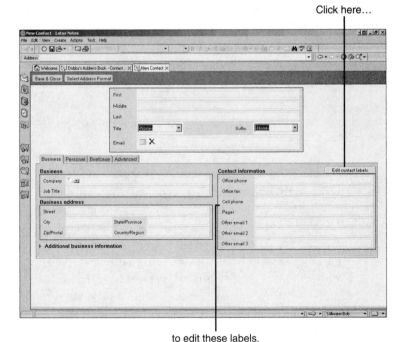

to edit these labels.

FIGURE 12.3

It is not required that you fill in every field in your contact information document. These phone number labels can be customized by clicking the Edit Contact Labels button discussed later in this lesson.

- On the **Personal** tabbed page you can add personal information about this contact, such as their home address, birthday, or anniversary (see Figure 12.4).

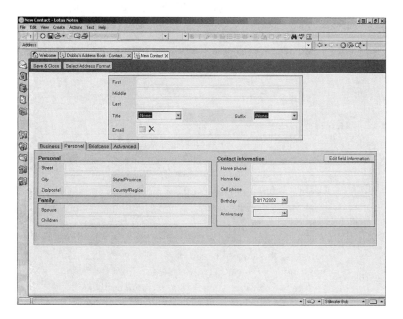

FIGURE 12.4
When you include a birthday on the Personal tab of a contact, that contact will be included in the Birthdays and Anniversaries view of your Address Book.

- The **Briefcase** tabbed page provides space to save photos, attach files, or add comments to your contact. For example, you could store a resume for a job candidate, a map or driving directions to a client's office, or a copy of an employee's review.

- The **Advanced** tabbed page allows you to categorize your contact so that it will show in the appropriate category when using the view **Contacts by Category**. If you want a contact to display under more than one category, separate categories with commas. Be consistent and watch your spelling, or you'll end up with several similar categories—Friends, Friend, Fiend—which makes it harder to find people. You can also choose which information, business or personal, you want displayed in your Preview Pane when previewing the contact information.

- When you add a new contact, click the **Save and Close** button on the Action bar to save this information in your address book.

NOTE

The form and information found for contacts in your Personal Address Book differs from the information you find on an individual in the Company Address Book. For example, the Company Address Book does not have a field for a Web address or birthday. You might want to record this information about a fellow co-worker, because lots of people have personal Web pages these days. In this case, instead of creating a new contact in your address book, copy that person from the Company Address Book into your Personal Address Book. Once added to your Personal Address Book, complete the information you want to keep. Remember, you don't need to copy the Company Address Book into your Personal Address Book for the mere purpose of being able to send email to a fellow employee. However, if a person's name or address changes in the Company Address Book, you will have erroneous information in your Personal Address Book. If you are a mobile Notes user, please be certain to complete Lessons 18 and 19 so you have a full understanding of address books and replication.

ADDING A PERSON FROM A MAIL MESSAGE

When you receive a mail message from a person who is not listed in your Personal Address Book, you can add that person. Open or select the mail message and then click the **Tools** button on the Action bar and select **Add Sender to Address Book**.

CREATING A MAILING LISTS

To send a mail message to more than one person, you can type each person's name, separated by a comma, or you can create a *mailing list*. To create a mailing list, follow these steps:

1. Select **Groups** from the Personal Address Book navigation pane.

2. Click the **New** button on the Action bar and choose **Group**.

3. The Basics section of the Group document is displayed as in Figure 12.5. Type a short, descriptive name for your group in the **Group Name** field.

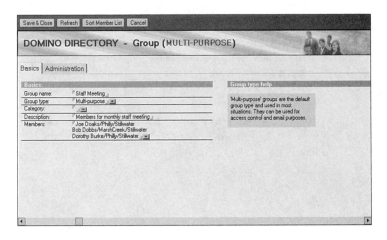

FIGURE 12.5
Mailing Lists can save time when you are addressing mail.

4. Click the small triangle to the right of the **Group Type** field and select **Mail Only** for your group. The other options, **Multipurpose, Access Control List Only,** and **Servers only,** are for use by your System Administrator.

5. Type a short description of the group in the Description field. Although this is not a mandatory field, it might remind you why you created this group.

6. Click the down arrow next to the field and select the names from your Personal Address Book.

TOO MUCH MAIL?

Lotus Notes saves a copy of your mail by default. Including yourself in a group results in your having two copies of a mail message, the one you saved and the one you received as a member of the group.

7. When you're done, click the **Save and Close** button.

CREATING GROUPS FROM MAIL

If you have a mail message open that includes a list of recipients, you can create a group for that list. Open the message and choose **Actions, Add Recipients, to new Group in Address Book** from the menu. A dialog box opens with a list of recipients checked. Click OK and a new document is created. Another way to create a Group document is to check multiple people in your Contacts view of your Address Book and choose **Tools, Copy into New Group** on the Action bar.

After you create the group, you can use it when you address memos. Simply type the name of the group in the To field (Quick address completes the name as you type), and Notes sends your email to all the people in the group. If a person drops out of the group or a new person is added, you can edit the group document by selecting it from the Groups view and clicking the **Edit Group** button on the Action bar. By using the group name when addressing your mail, you can save a lot of typing.

QUICK MEMO TO GROUP

To quickly address a memo to a group, open the group view, highlight the group, and click **Write Memo**.

Some groups need to exist only for the length of a project on which you're working. When you need to remove a group from your Personal Address Book, select it from the **Groups** view and click the **Delete Group** button on the Action bar.

CUSTOMIZING THE ADDRESS BOOK

By default, Notes sorts contacts in views by their first name. To change this default so you view contacts by last name, follow these steps:

1. Choose **Actions**, **Edit Address Book Preferences** from the menu or **Tools**, **Preferences** from the Action bar.

2. Select **Display names by default in Contact form/views(s):Lastname Firstname.**

3. Click **Update All Entries** to change existing entries as well as new entries.

4. Click **Save and Close**.

For any contact, you can customize field names (Lotus calls them *labels*) on the Business and Personal tabs. Perhaps you want the *Other email 1* label to say *Home email*. To do this, click the **Edit Contact Labels** button near the top of the Contact Information section and rename the labels.

FIGURE 12.6
When you click Edit Contact Labels, a dialog box appears. There, you can use field name suggestions provided by Notes in a drop-down menu, or you can type in your own names for fields.

You can also customize a contact's address format. Notes provides seven different internally accepted formats for addressing mail. These formats are applied when you print labels from your address book. To apply an address format, open a contact and click the **Select Address Format** button on the Action bar. Choose the address format you prefer and **Save and Close** the contact.

PRINTING FROM YOUR ADDRESS BOOK

You can print an alphabetical list of your contacts with their phone numbers and email addresses, and you can also print address or shipping labels in various sizes. Printing lists and labels for address books is available for local address books only, so if you need to print from your Domino Directory, you must replicate the directory to your hard drive or copy the Domino Directory into your address book. For more information on replication, see Lesson 18, "Understanding Replication." To print from your address book, follow these steps:

1. Open your Address Book and select the contact names you want to print by placing a checkmark in the margin. If you want to select your entire address book, choose, **Edit, Select All** from the menu.

2. With your contacts selected, choose **File, Print** from the menu. The Print dialog box appears as shown in Figure 12.7.

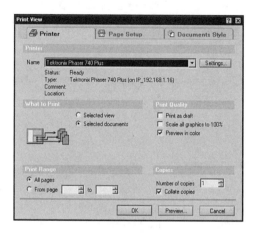

FIGURE 12.7
Make certain the correct printer and tray for the printer are selected when you want to print labels from your Address Book.

3. Click the **Documents Style** tab. To print a list, under the How to Print Each Document option, choose how many contacts to print on each page. You can click the **Preview** button to preview your options.

4. To print labels or a list other than the standard default list of contacts, go to the **Format Each Document Using** section and click the **Alternate Form** radio button.

5. A drop-down menu appears in which you can select the labels or lists you want (see Figure 12.8). There are choices here for both address labels and shipping labels.

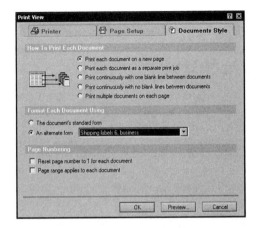

FIGURE 12.8
Various formats are available for shipping and address labels.

6. Optionally specify page-numbering options.

7. Optionally click the Page Setup tab and specify additional page formatting as well as paper source (important when you are creating labels). Click **OK** when you are finished with your selections, and Notes will print your list or labels.

In this lesson, you learned about the address books and how to use your Personal Address Book for creating contacts and groups as well as lists and labels. In the next lesson, you learn how to navigate the Web using Lotus Notes.

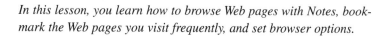

Lesson 13
Navigating the Web

In this lesson, you learn how to browse Web pages with Notes, book-mark the Web pages you visit frequently, and set browser options.

Setting Browser Preferences

You can browse Internet or intranet pages with Notes, or you can use other browser applications, such as Netscape Navigator or Microsoft Internet Explorer. A major advantage to using Notes as your browser is that Notes gives you the ability to store copies of Web pages as documents in a Notes database. There are two ways that Notes can be configured to browse the Web:

- Notes can retrieve the pages directly. In this setup, the Web pages retrieved by Notes are stored locally, and only you can view them.

- A Domino server, called the InterNotes server, retrieves the Web pages. In this setup, the retrieved Web pages are stored on the server, and any user with access to that server can view the pages.

You need to consult your Domino Administrator to find out which way your organization is set up to retrieve Web pages.

To retrieve Web pages directly from the Notes client, you must have either a direct or a proxy connection to the Internet. A direct connection uses TCP/IP and a dial-up modem or leased line. Transmission Control Protocol/Internet Protocol (TCP/IP) is a network protocol that is used for the Internet (a *network protocol* defines how computers on a network communicate with one another). A proxy connection uses TCP/IP and a proxy server that connects to the Internet for you (instead of you going directly to an Internet service provider, or ISP) and retrieves the Web pages for you. Check with your Domino Administrator to find out what type of connection you have.

Configure your connections in your Location documents (if your Administrator hasn't already set that up for you). The Location documents, which are stored in your Personal Address Book, tell Notes where your computer is (at home, traveling, in the office), on which server your mail file is located, and how your computer connects to that server (over a Local Area Network, over a modem, or isn't connected).

Each of your Location documents contains a setting for the Web browser you want to use. You might use a different method of connecting when you are in the office (such as a proxy server) than you would when working at home and disconnected from the office network (such as a modem connection directly to an ISP). Therefore, you need to specify which Web browser you want to use for the current location. You only need to do that once for each location you use. (You'll learn more about Location documents in Lesson 19, "Using Notes Remotely.")

To retrieve pages directly, and specify Notes as your Web browser, follow these steps:

1. Choose **File**, **Preferences**, **Location Preferences** from the menu to open the Location document (or click the **Location** button on the Status bar and choose **Edit Current**).

2. When the Location document opens, click the **Internet Browser** tab (see Figure 13.1).

3. From the Internet browser list, select **Notes** as your browser.

4. Select **from Notes workstation** from the Retrieve/open pages list.

5. Click the **Save & Close** button on the Action bar.

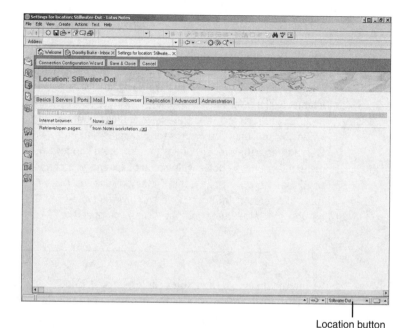

Location button

FIGURE 13.1
Choose the Web browser you want to use for this Location from the Internet browser list.

If you need to connect using a proxy server, go to the **Basics** tab in the Location document and enter the name or IP (Internet Protocol) address in the **Proxy** field (supplied to you by your Administrator) for the proxy server (each computer on the Internet has a unique address that is the IP address).

To make Notes your default browser for all locations, choose **File, Preferences, User Preferences** from the menu. From the Additional Options list, select **Make Notes the Default Web Browser on My System**. Then, click **OK**.

NOTE

To use Microsoft Internet Explorer, Netscape Navigator, or other software as your Web browser, you must have that software installed on your computer. Confirm this and choose **File, Preferences, Location Preferences** to open your current Location document. Select the **Internet Browser** tab. In the **Internet Browser** field, choose the browser you want to use—**Netscape Navigator**, **Microsoft Internet Explorer**, or **Other** (for **Other**, you must specify the path for the browser). Click the **Save & Close** button. When you use these other browser programs and enter a Web address, the browser opens in a separate window. If instead you choose **Notes with Internet Explorer**, you can continue to browse from within Notes but use the features of Microsoft Internet Explorer. However, you won't get the special features you have when you specify Notes as your browser.

To browse the Internet using an InterNotes server, choose **File, Preferences, Location Preferences** from the menu to open the current Location document. Click the **Internet Browser** tab. From the Internet Browser list, select **Notes** as your browser. Select **From InterNotes Server** from the Retrieve/Open Pages list.

Then, click the **Servers** tab. Specify the name of the InterNotes server you'll be using (ask your Domino Administrator) in the **InterNotes Server** field. Click **Save & Close** when you are finished.

OPENING WEB PAGES

There are several ways to open Web pages from within Notes, but the easiest is to enter the URL (Uniform Resource Locator) into the **Address** box on the toolbar (see Figure 13.2). Press Enter, and Notes retrieves the page. It isn't necessary to enter the complete address, because Notes assumes the http:// part of the URL. Just start the address with the www (when applicable) when you enter it, such as www.takeawalk.com. If you have visited that page previously, you can click the down arrow at the right end of the Address field and select the URL from the list.

Address box

Figure 13.2   *Open Web pages by entering the URL in the Address box, just as you do in many browsers.*

Use Bookmarks to mark your most frequently visited Web pages. This will save you time in opening those Web sites in the future. To create a Bookmark, right-click on the Window tab for the Web page and select **Create Bookmark** from the context menu to open the Add Bookmark dialog box. Give the bookmark a name and select a folder in which to store it (or put it on the Bookmark bar). Click **OK**.

URL addresses you see in emails or other Notes documents are *hotspots.* When you click on one of these hotspots, the Web page opens.

TIP

To have Notes automatically create hotspots from URLs that appear in rich text fields of Notes documents, choose **File, Preferences, User Preferences** from the menu. On the Basics page, select **Make Internet URLs (http:// ...) into Hotspots** from the Additional Options list. When the hotspots appear in the documents, click them to open the URL. To detect text as a URL in the rich text field, however, it must begin with http://. Documents in edit mode must be closed and reopened for the URL to become a hotspot.

Like any browser, Notes has tools to help you navigate the Internet. These same tools work when navigating Notes—databases, documents, views, or Web pages. These tools are on the Navigation toolbar (see Figure 13.3). Table 13.1 explains their uses.

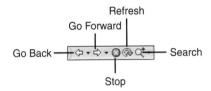

FIGURE 13.3
Navigate though Web pages using these buttons.

TABLE 13.1 Navigation Buttons for Web Pages

Name	Description
Go Back	Takes you to the previous page you had open when you click once. Click the down arrow next to the button to see a list of where you have been and select one to revisit.
Go Forward	After you have gone backward, clicking Go Forward takes you to the next page after the one you're on. Click the down arrow next to the button to see a list of where you have been and select one to revisit.
Stop	Stops loading the page you requested from the Internet.
Refresh	Reloads a Web page directly from the Internet.
Search	Click to search for text in a view or a Web page. Click the down arrow next to the button to search for people or databases, or to start an Internet search engine such as Lycos or Yahoo!

Storing Retrieved Pages

When you use Notes to retrieve Web pages directly, the pages are stored in the Personal Web Navigator database located on your local drive. If you use an InterNotes server to retrieve Web pages, the pages are stored in the Server Web Navigator database located on that server. The InterNotes server is shared by many users, so the Server Web Navigator database will also contain pages that have been visited by other users.

NOTE

If you are using Notes with Internet Explorer as your browser, you can automatically store pages in the Personal Web Navigator database as you view them. With a Web page open, choose **Actions, Internet Options** from the menu. Select the **Size options** tab and then select **Automatically store pages for disconnected use**. Click **Save and Close**. To save pages manually, open a Web page and choose **Actions, Internet Options** from the menu. On the Size options tab, select **Manually store pages for disconnected use**. Click **Save and Close**. When you are ready to save a page you have open, choose **Actions, Keep Page** from the menu.

You need to specify how often stored pages should be updated. From the menu, choose **File, Preferences, Location Preferences**. When the current Location document opens, select the **Advanced** tab, and then click the **Web Retriever** tab (see Figure 13.4).

Select an option from Update cache:

- **Never**—Select this option if you never want to update your stored Web pages. This is the default setting.

- **Once Per Session**—Choose this option to update stored Web pages once per Notes session.

- **Every Time**—Select to update stored Web pages each time you open one. This is especially important when you need up-to-date information every time you open a page (such as with stock prices).

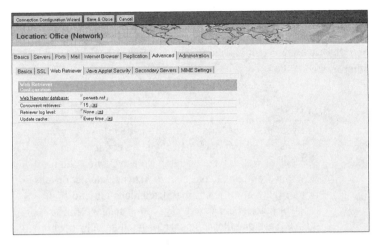

FIGURE 13.4
*Messages about Web retrieval are stored in your Notes log, along with the daily activities Notes performs. For Retriever log level, select **None** to have no messages sent (the default) about Web retrieval, **Terse** to send minimal messages, or **Verbose** to send all messages.*

Click the **Save & Close** button on the Action bar to save your choices.

TIP

How many parts of a Web page do you want to retrieve at once? Do you want to retrieve the text, images, and video all at the same time? You can set Notes to retrieve more than one at a time by choosing **File, Preferences, Location Preferences** from the menu, clicking the **Advanced** tab, selecting the **Web Retriever** tab, and then selecting a number in the **Concurrent Retrievers** field (15 is the default). However, the more retrievals you have working at the same time, the more computer memory you use, and the slower your computer will be in downloading pages.

Viewing Pages Offline

To browse when you are disconnected from the Internet, change your Location document (or switch to a location that is disconnected, such as Island). Choose **File**, **Preferences**, **Location Preferences** from the menu to open the current Location document. Select the **Internet Browser** tab. From the Retrieve/open pages field, choose **work offline** and click **OK**. Then, click the **Save & Close** button on the Action bar.

QUICK EDIT!

Quickly edit a location document by clicking the location in the status bar and choosing **Edit Current** from the pop-up menu. To switch locations, select a different location from the pop-up menu.

With **work offline** selected, Notes will only retrieve pages from the Personal Web Navigator or Server Web Navigator database. Notes won't retrieve pages from the Web. You will have to reconnect and change the setting in the Location document before you can retrieve new or updated pages.

If you switch to the Island (disconnected) location, you should use this setup so you can continue viewing Web pages you've stored.

CAUTION

To browse pages stored in the Server Web Navigator database while disconnected, you'll have to make a replica of the database (see Lesson 18 to learn about replication). Do that just before you disconnect to ensure you have the most up-to-date copy of the database.

FORWARDING AND MAILING PAGES

Forwarding a Web page sends the body of the Web page to the recipient (be sure you also include the URL). That way, the recipient can immediately see why the page caught your attention, making it more likely that the person will visit the page. However, to ensure that the person can access all the features of the page, you should forward the *URL* instead of the page.

To forward a page, open the Web page and choose **Actions, Forward** from the menu. Then select **Forward copy of this page**. In the new Mail Memo that opens, enter or select the names of the recipients in the To field. Type any necessary comments, and then click **Send**.

CAUTION

The page you forward might not look exactly as you saw it on the Web if you specified **Notes with Internet Explorer** as your browser and you forward a copy of a page to a user who uses Notes as his browser. The contents of the page are converted from HTML to rich text, so some differences might occur. Also, when using Notes with Internet Explorer, you are able to forward URLs using the FILE protocol, which you can't do in Notes.

To forward a URL, start from the open Web page and choose **Actions, Forward** from the menu. You then select **Forward bookmark to this page** and click **OK**. You enter the names of the recipients in the To field of the new memo (see Figure 13.5) or select them from the Address Book. Type any comments you want to accompany the URL, and then click **Send**.

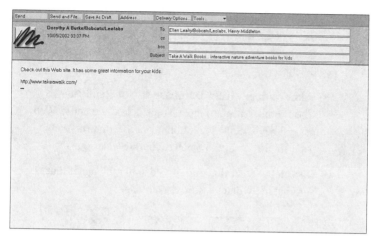

FIGURE 13.5
This Mail Memo forwards the URL of a Web page to two recipients. When the memo is received, the recipient can click the URL to open the Web page.

PERFORMING HOUSEKEEPING

Storing all the Web pages you visit could result in a very large database file. At some time, you'll have to remove some of those files. One way to do this is to use the Housekeeping agent to automatically delete stored Web pages. When enabled, this agent runs daily at 1:00 a.m. To enable Housekeeping, follow these steps:

1. Open a Web page.

2. Choose **Actions, Internet Options** from the menu.

3. Click the **Size Options** tab (see Figure 13.6), and select one of these options:

   • **Reduce Full Pages to Links If Not Read Within—** Select this option to have Notes delete the contents of the Web page but save the URL so you can still open the page on the Web. Then specify the number of days that the Web page should be in the database before deletion.

- **Remove Pages from Database If Not Read In—** Choose this option to have Notes delete the entire Web page. Then specify the number of days that the Web page should be in the database before deletion.

- **Disable—**Select this option to disable the agent that automatically deletes stored Web pages.

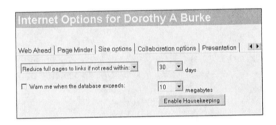

FIGURE 13.6
Set your housekeeping options to reduce the size of Web pages that haven't been read recently or to delete those pages.

4. **(Optional)** If you want to be warned when the database gets to a certain size, select **Warn Me When the Database Exceeds** and then specify a size in megabytes.

5. Click **Enable Housekeeping**.

6. Click **Save and Close**.

You must enable scheduled local agents first in order to use the Housekeeping agent. If you've done this once, you need not do it again. If you've not enabled scheduled agents, choose **File, Preferences, User Preferences,** and place a check mark next to **Enable scheduled local agents.** Click **OK.** Remember that agents will only run when your computer is turned on with Notes running.

If you prefer, you can delete Web pages manually. You'll need to perform both House Cleaning and File Archives (see the following bullets) when you are manually deleting because House Cleaning deletes documents and File Archives deletes actual files (Word docs, zip files and so forth) that have been accessed via the Web and stored. Open the Personal Web Navigator or your local replica of the Server Web Navigator and do one of the following:

- Select **Other, House Cleaning** in the Navigation pane to display a list of documents sorted in descending order by document size (these include Web pages and files associated with them, such as cookies and stylesheets). Select the documents you want to remove, and then click **Delete** on the Action bar. Notes deletes the selected documents.

- Select **Other, File Archive** if you want to delete files based on file name. Notes displays a list of files, sorted alphabetically by file name (although you can click the sorting arrows in the File Size column heading to sort the view by file size). Select the files you want to remove, and then click **Delete** on the Action bar. Notes deletes the selected files.

In this lesson you learned how to use Notes to browse Web pages, how pages are saved, and how to perform housekeeping. You also learned how to forward a Web page or its URL in a mail memo. In the next lesson you learn to manage documents in Notes databases.

LESSON 14

Managing Documents

In this lesson, you learn how to refresh views, edit documents, and view unread documents. You also learn how to find and replace text in a document and in a database.

REFRESHING VIEWS

It is not uncommon for Notes users to have several databases open at one time; the mail database is usually one of them. Over time (minutes, hours), new documents are added to databases that do not appear in the View pane unless you occasionally update, or refresh, the view. Refreshing the view forces Notes to present a current, accurate listing of documents that have been added to the database since you opened the view. This is a similar process to refreshing a Web page.

Notes tells you when new documents have been added to a database or when documents have been edited by placing a Refresh icon on the View pane. If the icon appears, click it, press *F9*, or click the Refresh icon found on the Navigation bar (see Figure 14.1) to refresh the view. If no Refresh icon appears in your View pane, it is not necessary to refresh the view.

The exception to the need to refresh is your mail database, which Notes refreshes automatically.

Refresh Navigation
Refresh icon   button

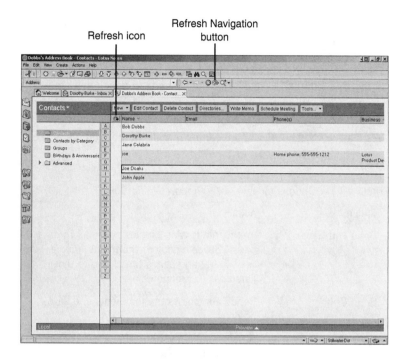

FIGURE 14.1
When you see the Refresh icon in your View pane, click it to refresh your view.

CAUTION

Depending on the database in which you are working, it is possible that you do not have editing rights to a document. If you need to but are unable to edit a document, contact your Domino system administrator.

EDITING DOCUMENTS

To edit a document, select the document and choose **Actions**, **Edit** from the menu. You also can press **Ctrl+E** to place the document in edit mode, or double-click the document while reading it. Depending on the database, you might also be presented with an **Edit Document** button in the Action bar.

When you finish editing a document, press the **Esc** key, or click the **X** in the Task Button. Depending on the database in which you are working, the Close Window dialog box (see Figure 14.2) or a Lotus Notes dialog box appears, asking if you want to save your changes (select **Yes**, **No**, or **Cancel**). If you are editing a Mail Memo, you might see other choices as described in Table 14.1.

TABLE 14.1   Options for the Close Window Dialog Box

Option	Action
Send and Save	Applicable to Mail Memos and mail in databases. Saves a copy of the memo in your Sent folder and sends the memo to those listed as the recipients.
Send Only	Sends a memo to the recipients and saves no copy.
Save Only	Saves a copy in your drafts folder; does not send the document.
Discard Changes	Exits the document and nothing is saved or mailed.
Cancel	Exits the dialog box and returns you to the document in edit mode.

EDITING SENT & RECEIVED MESSAGES

Because it does not serve any purpose, you probably will not be modifying mail that has already been sent or new mail that you receive. If you want to copy all the text from one message into a new memo, calendar, or To Do document, select the document in the view and then use the **Copy Into** button on the Action bar. Remember, too, that you can forward messages, sending a message you've received on to another person.

FIGURE 14.2
Pressing Esc or closing a Mail Memo window while editing or creating a memo brings up the Close Window dialog box.

VIEWING UNREAD DOCUMENTS

To view only documents or messages you have *not* read, choose **View, Show, Unread Only** from the menu. This menu command is a toggle—when you want to see all the documents in the view (including read documents), choose **View, Show, Unread Only** again and remove the check mark next to **Unread Only**.

FINDING AND REPLACING TEXT IN A DOCUMENT

You can easily find words or phrases within a Notes document or mail message. You can find text, or you can find and replace text (depending on your access level to that document). After you find text, you can replace it quickly and effortlessly by using the same Find and Replace dialog box.

FIND OR SEARCH?

Use Find or Find and Replace when you are searching for text within a document. To search an entire database for documents containing text, see "Searching for Text in a Database" later in this lesson.

To find or replace specific text in a document, follow these steps:

1. If you are Finding only, the document must be open. If you want to Find and Replace, the document must be in edit

mode. Choose **Edit, Find/Replace** from the menu. The **Find Text in Document** dialog box is displayed as pictured in Figure 14.3.

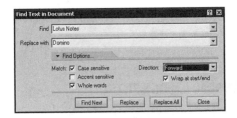

FIGURE 14.3
You can find or replace words or phrases anywhere in a document.

I CAN'T REPLACE THE TEXT!

Whether or not you can replace text in a document depends on two things: First, you must be in edit mode, and second, you must have sufficient access rights to edit that document. If you are working in your mail database, you are the manager of the database and can, therefore, replace whatever you want. If you're working in a database other than mail, it is possible that you do not have rights to edit documents, particularly if you didn't create the documents. For more information on Notes and Domino security, see Appendix A, "Understanding Security and Access Rights."

2. In the **Find** text box, enter the text you want to find.

3. (**Optional**) In the **Replace with** text box, enter the text you want to substitute for the found text.

4. (**Optional**) Click the twistie to the left of Find Options. Choose any of the following options:

Case sensitive—Searches for the character string that matches the case exa8ctly, as with names of programs or people.

Accent sensitive—Tells Notes to include diacritical accent marks (such as those used in foreign languages).

Whole Words—Finds the character string you entered only when a space precedes and follows the word. For example, if you enter *the* and do not choose Whole Word, Notes finds such words as *their*, *there*, and *other*.

Wrap around—Searches the entire document regardless of your cursor position at the time you start the search. If not selected, Notes will search from the cursor position forward or backward, depending on the selection of **Find forwards** or **Find backwards.**

5. Click the **Find Next** button to find the next occurrence of the word in the text. Choose the **Find Previous** button to find the previous occurrence of the word. If it finds a match, Notes highlights the word in the text and leaves the Find and Replace dialog box open.

6. (**Optional**) Click the **Replace** button to replace the highlighted text that Notes found with the text you typed in the Replace text box. Or, if you're sure you want to replace all occurrences, click the **Replace All** button to replace all occurrences automatically.

7. (**Optional**) Click **Find Next** or **Find Previous** (Find Previous appears after you have used Find Next and does not appear in Figure 14.3) to skip this occurrence and find the next occurrence of the specified text. You can click **Replace and Find Next,** which appears after you have found the first occurrence (and therefore does not appear in Figure 14.3) to replace the found text and jump to the next occurrence.

8. Click **Close** to close the dialog box.

SHORTCUT   Press **Ctrl+G** to find the word or phrase again without opening the Find and Replace dialog box. Notes remembers what you entered in the Find and Replace dialog box the last time, and it finds that text again.

SEARCHING FOR TEXT IN A DATABASE

Another way to find information in a document is Quick Search, which is a great way to find information in a view, such as your Mail Inbox view.

To use Quick Search, open the view you want to search and begin typing the word you want to find. Notes searches the first sorted column of the view, not the entire document contents, for the documents that match in the database.

Another kind of search available in Notes is a full-text search, in which you use the Search Builder. This type of search looks through the contents of the documents in a database, without having to open documents. To perform a full-text search, the database must first be indexed and contain a full-text index. A full-text index is a special file created by Notes that creates an index to the contents of documents. If a database has been full-text indexed, it is indicated so on the Search bar. To view the Search bar, choose **View**, **Search this View** on the menu. With full-text-indexed databases, you can do the following:

- Create search formulas to find documents

- Save search formulas to reuse later

To use the Search Builder, follow these steps:

1. In database view, choose View, Search this View. The Search bar appears above the view pane.

2. Enter a word or phrase in the **Search for** text box.

3. Click the **Search** button. All the documents that contain the word or phrase are displayed in the view pane (see Figure 14.4).

4. Click the **Clear Results** button to start a new search and display all the documents in the database.

CAUTION

> If your database is not indexed, create a full-text index by double-clicking the orange **Not Indexed** indicator on the Search bar or click the **More** button on the Search bar, then click the **Create Index** button that appears on the expanded more page. Accept the defaults for creating the index and click **OK**. To learn more about full text indexing and the choices found in the Full Text Index dialog box, search Lotus Notes Help for *create index*.

You also can set search criteria when you use the Search bar. To do so, click the **More** button at the right end of the Search bar (see Figure 14.4).

- **Conditions**—Search by date, author, field, form, or word combinations. In the multiple word dialog box you can find ALL or ANY word occurrences. If you want to find all words listed (documents that contain the word *blue* and *red*), choose **ALL**. If you want to find either of the words listed (documents that contain the word *blue* or the word *red*), choose **ANY**. The **Fill Out Example** button assists your search for words by giving you a sample of the form to fill out.

- **Use Word Variants**—Includes variants, such as plurals, in the search. For example, if you enter the word *network*, Notes finds *networks*, *networking*, and so on.

Search bar   Search results   Index indicator

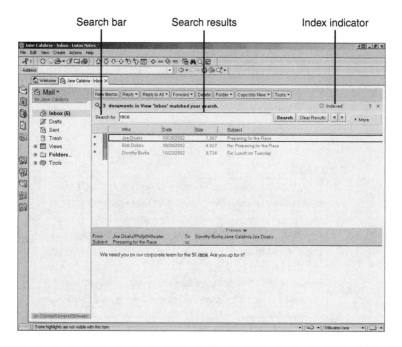

FIGURE 14.4
Notes lists the documents that contain the search text.

- **Sort Results by**—You can choose how you want the documents presented to you in the view.

- **Sort by Relevance**—Lists the documents with the most occurrences of the word first.

- **Save Search**—Displays the Save Search dialog box in which you can name the search so that you can use it again. After you save a search, you can reload it by clicking on the **Load Search** button. The search will automatically be carried out.

- **Delete Saved Search**—(An option found in the Load Search button.) Displays the Delete Saved Search dialog box from which you select saved searches and delete those you no longer use.

In this lesson, you learned how to refresh views, edit documents, and view unread documents. You also learned how to find and replace text in a document and how to search a database using the Search bar. In the next lesson, you learn how to edit and format text and fields.

LESSON 15

Editing and Formatting Text and Fields

In this lesson, you learn about text fields; how to select, move, and copy text; how to format text and paragraphs; how to set page breaks; and how to use the permanent pen.

SELECTING TEXT

Before you can copy, move, delete, or format text in a document, you must select it. The quickest and easiest method of selecting text in a document is to click and drag the mouse cursor across the text you want to select. When text is selected, it appears in reverse video, as shown in Figure 15.1.

If you selected too much text or you didn't mean to select text at all, click the mouse anywhere in the document to deselect the text. Alternatively, you can press the right or left arrow on the keyboard.

SHORTCUTS

Double-click any single word to select just that one word. Position your cursor in the left margin of a rich text field, click once to select a line of text, and click twice to select a paragraph.

Click here...

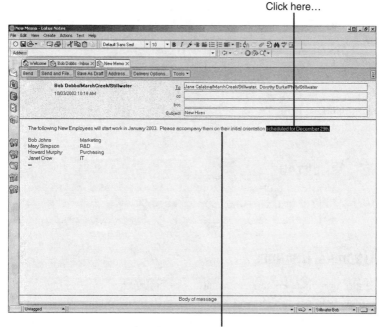

...then drag here and release mouse button.

FIGURE 15.1
Click and drag the mouse to quickly select text.

MOVING AND COPYING TEXT

You can move text from one part of the document to another part of
the same document or from one document to another. You also can
copy text between documents or within the same document. Follow
these steps to copy or move text:

1. Select the text you want to move or copy.

2. Choose **Edit, Cut** if you want to move the text, or choose
   Edit, Copy if you want to make a duplicate of the text. The
   text is copied or moved to the Windows Clipboard.

3. Reposition the cursor where you want to place the text (it can be in the same document or in another document).

   If you want to place the cut or copied text in another document, use the Window menu to switch back to the database or to another open document.

4. Choose **Edit, Paste**, and the copied or cut text appears at the insertion point.

SHORTCUT

> If you prefer to work from the keyboard, press **Ctrl+X** to cut text, **Ctrl+C** to copy text, and **Ctrl+V** to paste text.

UNDOING CHANGES

Undoing a change such as formatting or cutting text cancels the effects you just applied and returns the document to its previous state. For example, if you cut some text and you didn't mean to, you can undo that action. The text is returned to its original location. To undo changes, choose **Edit, Undo** or press **Ctrl+Z**.

You must choose to Undo an action before you perform another. Because Notes can remember only one action at a time, each new action replaces the last one.

CAN'T UNDO

> Not all changes and edits can be undone. If the Undo command is dimmed, you cannot undo your previous command.

Types of Fields

Notes forms contain several types of fields. Some are automatically
filled in and others are fields in which you enter information. Notes
fields in which you enter data are easily identified because they are
the white boxes—usually to the right or below the static text that
describes the field—where you type in information, as you have seen
in the heading of the Mail Memo form.

The following list describes the common field types you find in Notes
database forms. Not all forms contain all of these elements.

- **Text Fields**—Fields in which you can enter words and sentences, usually titles or topics. You cannot format text in a
  text field.

- **Rich Text Fields**—Fields in which you can enter text, import
  text, import graphics such as .PCX or .TIFF files, and attach
  files. The body of the Mail Memo is a rich text document.
  You can apply both text and paragraph formatting in rich text
  fields.

- **Keyword Fields**—Fields in which you select choices from a
  list. The Company field in the Business Card is a keyword
  field. Depending on the database design, you might be able to
  enter or even add your own keywords.

- **Date/Time Fields**—Very often, these fields are automatically
  filled by Notes, using your computer's clock. Most time
  fields display hour and minute, while most date fields display
  month, date, and year.

- **Number Fields**—Fields that can contain only numbers, such
  as currency or quantities.

To enter information into a field, click inside of the field and begin
typing. To move from field to field on a form, press the **Tab** key.

Fields within the mail database are rarely fixed-length fields, which means they grow in size as you type information into them. In some cases, a database designer can make a field fixed-length to keep the integrity of the data consistent. For example, he might design the area code field to accept only three characters.

For the most part, information that you place in Notes fields can be copied, moved, or deleted as you would in any word processor. However, as stated above, the ability to format text and paragraphs in a field is reserved for rich text fields.

FORMATTING TEXT

You can change character formatting in any rich text field to make your documents more interesting or attractive, or to emphasize important text. As pictured in Figure 15.2, character formatting includes working with the following characteristics:

- **Font**—Apply a typeface to text in the document. For example, you can make a title stand out by applying a different typeface to it. You are limited to the fonts available in your operating system.

- **Size**—Apply a size to the text to increase or decrease the size of the printed or displayed text. Typically, larger text (say, 24-point size) commands more attention, and smaller text (10-point, for example) is reserved for details.

- **Style**—Apply special text formatting—plain, bold, italic, underline, strikethrough, subscript, superscript, shadow, emboss, or extrude—to add emphasis and clarity to your document.

- **Color**—Apply color to text to further define the text in your document.

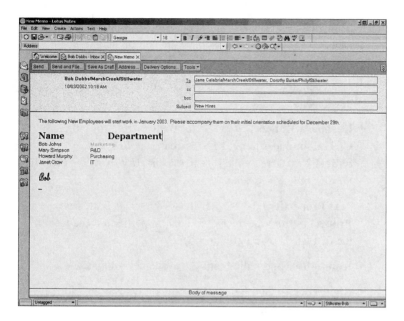

FIGURE 15.2
Character formatting makes your documents more attractive and easier to read if you don't overdo the number of fonts and types of formatting.

PLAIN ENGLISH

Font/Typeface—A font is a set of characters in one style and size. Times New Roman, Courier, and Helv are common fonts, and Helv10 is a different font than Helv12.

Point—A measurement of type; there are 72 points in an inch. Body text is generally 10- or 12-point, and headlines or titles are usually 14-, 18-, or 24-point.

Select your text before you apply formatting. There are several methods of applying text formatting after you have selected it:

- **Status bar**—Click directly on the font name and font size and select your new choices from the pop-up lists.

- **Menu**—Press **Alt+T** on your keyboard to open the **Text** menu bar. Select your character formatting from the pull-down menu.

- **Keyboard Hotkeys**—**Ctrl+B** for Bold, **Ctrl+I** for Italic, **Ctrl+U** for underlining, **F2** to increase the font size, **Shift+F2** to decrease the font size. *Hint: Hotkeys are listed in the Text pull-down menu.*

- **Text Properties box**—Press **Ctrl+K** or select **Text, Text Properties** from the menu bar. Font properties are changed in the first tab as seen in Figure 15.3.

- **Icons**—Bold and Italic **Icons** are available by default.

- **Right-click**—Choose the most common types of text formatting from the shortcut menu.

FIGURE 15.3
When you are done formatting your text, close the Properties Box by clicking on the X in the upper-right corner.

HIGHLIGHT THE GOOD POINTS

To add some extra emphasis to existing text, add some color to the line. Choose **Text, Highlighter** from the menu and then select your color: yellow, blue, or pink. As you drag your mouse cursor over text, it is highlighted in the color you choose. Don't forget to turn it off when you are done by choosing **Text**, **Highlighter** and deselecting the highlighter.

FORMATTING PARAGRAPHS

You apply paragraph formatting for the same reasons as you apply text formatting—that is, to add emphasis and clarity to your documents. It is helpful to view the ruler in Notes as you work. To display the ruler, place your cursor in rich text field (such as the body of a memo) and choose **View, Ruler** from the menu. As pictured in Figure 15.4, paragraph formatting includes working with the following characteristics:

Alignment—Move the paragraph to the left margin or right margin, center it between the left and right margins, fully justify it to both the left and right margins, or continue it past the right margin without word wrapping.

Margins—Set ruler measurements for your left and right margin. You can also indent or outdent the first line of a paragraph or the entire paragraph.

Tab Stops—Set ruler measurements for tab placement. Choices include left tabs, right tabs, centered tabs, and decimal place tabs.

Line Spacing—Set the amount of space you want between lines of text in your document. Choices include

- **Interline**—Determines the space between the lines of text within a paragraph.

- **Above**—Determines extra space added above a paragraph.

- **Below**—Determines extra space added below a paragraph.

- **Single, 1 1/2, or Double**—Sets the spacing for the selected paragraph.

- **Lists**—Extremely helpful for adding emphasis to documents, each item on the list is preceded by sequential numbers, small black dots, check boxes, square boxes, or circles.

Ruler

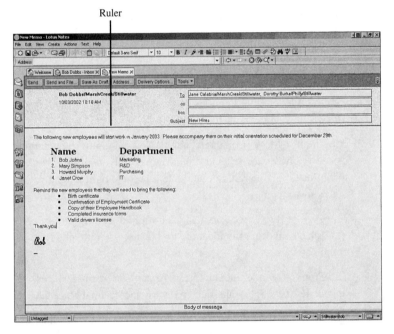

FIGURE 15.4
Very effective documents are created when you combine both character and paragraph formatting.

Like formatting text, you select your paragraph before you apply formatting. There are several methods of applying paragraph formatting after you have selected it:

- **Menu**—Press **Alt+T** on your keyboard to open the **Text** menu bar. Select your individual paragraph formatting from the pull-down menu.

- **Keyboard Hotkeys**—**F8** for Indent, **Shift+F8** for Outdent. *Hint: Hotkeys are listed in the Text pull-down menu.*

- **Text Properties box**—Press **Ctrl+K** or select **Text, Text Properties** from the menu bar. Paragraph properties are changed in the second and third tab, as seen in Figure 15.5.

- **Icons**—Alignment, Indent, Outdent, and List Icons are available by default.

- **Right-click**—Choose the most common types of paragraph formatting from the shortcut menu.

FIGURE 15.5
Click on the Paragraph tab of the text formatting properties box to select paragraph formatting options. Click on the third tab to set paragraph margins.

PLAIN ENGLISH

Paragraph

In Notes, a paragraph is defined as text contained between hard paragraph returns (which you create by pressing **Enter**). A paragraph can contain several sentences, several words, one word or letter, or it can even be a blank line. To see your paragraphs as you type, choose **View, Show, Hidden Characters**. To maintain formatting options but put a return within a paragraph (called a soft return) press **Shift + Enter**.

TIP

If you find you frequently use the same formatting options but not frequently enough to change the defaults of the program, create *styles* for this purpose. Search the Notes Help database to learn how to save and reuse your formatting preferences in styles.

USING PAGE BREAKS

Notes automatically inserts page breaks but you can insert your own page breaks to organize your documents.

CAN'T SEE BREAKS?

If you cannot see the page breaks that Notes creates, choose **View, Show, Page Breaks**.

To insert a page break, follow these steps:

1. Position the insertion point where you want a page break.

2. Choose **Create, Page Break**. Notes displays a thin black line across the page to show the page break.

THE PERMANENT PEN

The permanent pen enables you to add text in a different color or font than the default font settings so that it stands out from the rest of the document. This is especially useful for collaborative projects because each user can work in a different color permanent pen; everyone can see who contributed to the document by the color of the text. This feature is easier to use when you want to apply the same text formatting to non-contiguous text that you've already typed, or when you are inserting new text into existing text such as comments. Permanent pen only works in a rich text field such as the body of a message. The default permanent pen is bold red text.

I DIDN'T SAY THAT

When a message or document is forwarded to you from another person, you can edit your copy of the original message. However, because it is not appropriate to modify the sender's text without her knowledge, use permanent pen to add your own comments before forwarding it on to anyone else.

To turn on the permanent pen, choose **Text, Permanent Pen, Use Permanent** or click the  **Permanent Pen** Icon. "Permanent Pen enabled" displays in the status bar at the bottom of your screen. Then, type the text you want to appear in the permanent pen style. To stop using the permanent pen and begin using normal text again, click the **Permanent Pen** Icon again, or remove the check mark next to **Use Permanent Pen** in the menu.

RUB IT OUT

Strikethrough text is used to mark text that you want to edit out (for example: ~~Exchange~~ Notes). To accomplish this with the permanent pen, first select the words you want to strike through. Then use the hotkey combination **Shift+Backspace** to mark the text.

To change the look of the permanent pen from the default bold red text, type some text and apply the formatting to that text. Then, select the text and choose **Text, Permanent Pen, Set Permanent Pen Style**. In setting the permanent pen formatting, you can set the font, the font color, and the size and style.

In this lesson, you learned about rich text fields; how to select, move, and copy text; how to apply character and paragraph formatting; how to set custom page breaks; and how to use the permanent pen. In the next lesson you learn how to create links, tables, and sections.

LESSON 16
Enhancing Documents

In this lesson, you learn how to create document, database, and view links, as well as tables and sections.

CREATING DOCUMENT, DATABASE, ANCHOR, AND VIEW LINKS

Links are pointers to other documents, views, or Lotus Notes databases. If you want to send a mail message and refer to a page in the Help database, you can create a document link in your mail message. When the recipient receives your mail, he can click the **Document Link** icon and see the page to which you are referring.

Links work the same way that hypertext works in the Help database, displaying underlined text that you click to open other documents, or by displaying an icon that represents the link. There are four types of Lotus Notes links that you can create and include in your mail messages or Lotus Notes documents (see Table 16.1).

It's important to understand that links only work when they are linked to documents, views, and databases to which others have access. If you link to a document that has been deleted or to a database not available to or accessible by the person to whom you are sending the link (such as your Mail database), it simply won't work.

TABLE 16.1 Types of Links

This Icon	Named	Does This
	Anchor Link	Connects to a *specific location* in the same document, or in a different document.
	Document Link	Connects to another Lotus Notes document. It can be a document in the same database or within an entirely different database. Double-clicking a document link results in the linked document appearing on the screen.
	View Link	Connects to a specific view in the current or different database.
	Database Link	Connects to another database opened at its default view.

CREATING DOCUMENT LINKS

The examples in this lesson create links from a Mail Memo to the Help database. Be sure to use the server copy of the Help database, not a local copy. If you have access to discussion databases or other types of Lotus Notes databases, try these exercises using those databases instead of the Help and mail databases.

To create a document link, follow these steps:

1. Begin a mail message by filling in the header (address, subject line, and so on) information.

2. In the body field of your message, type a sentence telling the recipient what information is in the document that's linked to your Mail Memo (this is a courtesy, not a requirement). You might type something such as **I'm learning how to create a document link. If you want to learn too, click here.**

3. Press the **spacebar** (or to create an arrow **-->** press spacebar, dash, dash, greater than sign) at the end of your sentence. Open the Favorites Navigator Pane using the Button bar to access other databases without exiting this mail message.

4. Click the **Help** database icon to open the database. Do a quick search for links. Click on the twistie to expand the Using in documents section. Double-click to open the Using **links, buttons, hotspots, and sections in documents** document.

5. With the Help document open, choose **Edit**, **Copy as Link**, **Document Link** from the menu.

6. You created your document link. The next step is to paste it into your mail message. Click on the New Memo task button to return to your memo.

7. Place your cursor at the end of your sentence, remembering to leave the blank space. Choose **Edit**, **Paste** to insert the Document Link icon into your mail message (see Figure 16.1).

8. Send your mail message. Press **Esc** to close the Help database, or click the **X** in the Notes Help task button.

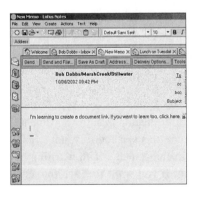

FIGURE 16.1
A document link is inserted at the position of your cursor when you create the link.

You can see the results of your document link by looking at the copy of the mail message you just sent. Open the Sent view of your mailbox and double-click the copy of the mail message you just created. If you want to display the name of the linked document, point at the document link icon and hold your mouse pointer there without clicking. A small hand appears, pointing at the link icon.

If you want to see the linked document, click the **Document Link** icon.

A WEAK LINK?

Remember, the success of links depends on the proper rights, or access, to a document or database. Be careful using document links with mail messages. For example, no one has access to your Inbox but you. You won't have success sending a document link to "Bob" so that he can see the message in your Inbox that you received from "Mary." Bob can't access your mailbox. In this case, you must forward Mary's message to Bob.

Lotus Notes automatically creates document links when you use the reply option of Mail. Look in your Inbox and locate a mail message you've received as a reply. It's easy to identify replies when you use the Discussion Thread view because the replies are indented. You can generally find them in your Inbox too because the subject line usually starts with **Re:**. Double-click to open a reply. You see a document link located at the end of the subject line. Lotus Notes automatically placed that document link; it points to the message to which this message is replying. Click the document link, and you can see the original message. This is an extremely helpful Mail tool, enabling you to easily work your way back through the path of mail messages.

TIP

> One quick way to see the linked document without click-
> ing on the document link icon is to choose **View**,
> **Document Link Preview** from the menu. The linked docu-
> ment appears in a Preview pane at the bottom of the
> screen.

To link to a particular location in a document, you should use an
anchor link.

1. Open the document you want to link to and put it in Edit
   mode.

2. Place your cursor at the beginning of the paragraph that you
   want to link to.

3. Choose **Edit, Copy as Link, Anchor Link** from the menu. A
   small anchor link icon appears next to the paragraph (it can
   only be seen in Edit mode).

4. Open the document where you want to place the link, making
   sure that it is in Edit mode.

5. Click where you want the link to appear, and then choose
   Edit, Paste from the menu.

CREATING A DATABASE LINK

A database link connects to the default view of another database. To
create a database link, choose **Edit, Copy as Link, Database Link**
from the menu while the database is opened.

CREATING VIEW LINKS

A view link works similarly to document links and database links. To
create a view link, follow the previous steps, but open the view to
which you want to link when you copy your view link. Choose **Edit,
Copy as Link, View Link** as your menu commands.

CREATING POP-UPS

A *text pop-up hotspot* displays pop-up text. This is handy when you send information to several people, and only parts of that information are needed by some of those people. For example, if you're including terms that won't be understood by all the recipients, you can put the definitions in text pop-ups. Those recipients who need the definitions can click a word and additional text appears with the explanation of the term, as seen in Figure 16.2.

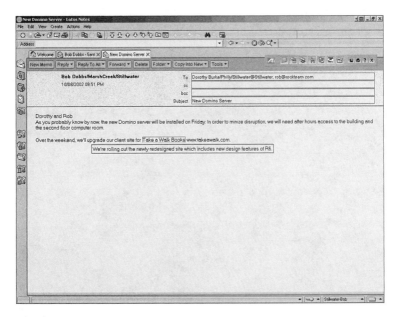

FIGURE 16.2
A text pop-up hotspot usually contains instructions, additional information, or directions.

A text pop-up can be created only in a rich text field, such as the body of your mail message. To create this kind of hotspot, follow these steps:

1. Begin a mail message by filling in the header information.

2. In the body of the mail message, type your message. Determine which word(s) you want to become the text hotspot word or phrase (Figure 16.3 uses *Take A Walk Books*).

3. Highlight that word or phrase by selecting it with your mouse. Choose **Create**, **Hotspot**, **Text Pop-Up** from the menu.

4. The HotSpot Pop-up Properties box appears, as shown in Figure 16.3.

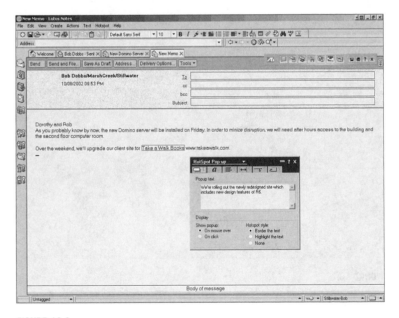

FIGURE 16.3
Additional help is available by clicking on the question mark in the upper-right corner of the HotSpot Pop-up Properties box.

5. In the Popup Text box, fill in the text you want to pop up when this hotspot is clicked. When you have finished typing the text, click the check mark.

6. Choose whether you want the pop-up to appear when the user holds the mouse over your text (**On mouse over**) or clicks on the pop-up (**On Click**).

7. Determine your hotspot appearance by selecting one of the Hotspot Style radio buttons.

8. Close the Properties box. Finish and send your message.

You can see the effects of your pop-up by looking at the copy of your message in Sent mail.

INSERTING TABLES

Tables offer an excellent way to organize data, and you can easily add tables to your mail messages. Figure 16.4 shows a mail message with a table inserted.

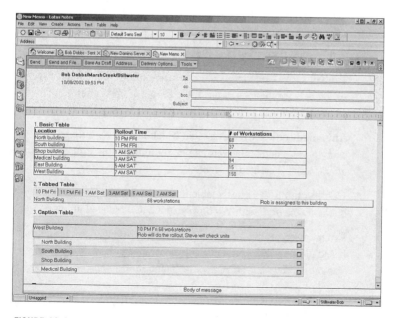

FIGURE 16.4

Here's a table created in three table types: 1. a Basic table, 2. a Tabbed table, and 3. a Caption table (which is a new table type in Notes 6).

To insert a table in your mail message, follow these steps:

1. Create a new memo.

2. Position your cursor in the body field where you want the table to appear.

3. Choose **Create, Table** or click the **Create Table** Icon. The Create Table dialog box appears (see Figure 16.5).I~Create Table dialog box>

4. Enter the number of Rows and Columns you want in your table. Check **Fixed Width** if you do not want the table to adjust to the width of the screen. Once you create a fixed-width table, you can set the column widths in the Table Properties box or drag the sizes of the columns using the ruler. To turn on the ruler, choose **View, Ruler** from the menu.

5. Select the table type:

Basic table—Add formatting options (colors, borders, and so forth) in the Table Properties box after you have created the table.

Tabbed table—Each row is presented as a different tabbed page. Add labels for the tabs in the Table Properties box after you have created the table.

Animated table—Creates a table which displays a different row every two seconds. Intervals can be set in the Table Properties box after you have created the table.

Caption table—Creates a table in which each row shows as a clickable caption, with Windows expand and reduce buttons.

Programmed table—Creates a table that presents a different row based on the value of a field. This is an advanced table in which you must create a field and so forth, and this table is beyond the scope of this book.

6. Click **OK**.

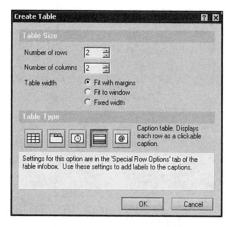

FIGURE 16.5
When you create a table, indicate the Table Type in the Create Table dialog box.

You can edit; insert columns and rows; and add borders, colors, and shading to tables. If you right-click an element of the table, the properties box appears, from which you can select properties for tables, rows, columns, or text. You can also edit a table by placing your cursor in the table and clicking the Table Properties SmartIcon on the SmartIcon Toolbar.

New table features of Notes 6 include placing tabs on any side of a tabbed table (see Figure 16.6), cutting and pasting an entire table of data, and copying a view as a table. To learn more about editing and formatting tables, search the Help database for *table*.

CREATING SECTIONS

Sections are helpful in making large documents more manageable. You can gather all the information on one topic into a section. Sections collapse into one-line paragraphs or expand to display all the text in the section, so a reader doesn't have to read sections that aren't of any interest. Figure 16.7 shows a document with both expanded and collapsed sections.

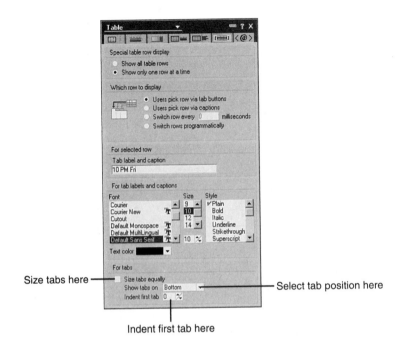

Size tabs here

Select tab position here

Indent first tab here

FIGURE 16.6
The Table Properties box contains options for table formatting such as the new option for displaying tabs on any side of a table.

When you gather text into a section, a small triangle appears to the left of the section head. To expand a section, click this triangle (called a *twistie*). Clicking again on the twistie collapses the section. To expand all the sections in a document, choose **View**, **Expand All Sections** from the menu. To collapse all sections, choose **View**, **Collapse All Sections** from the menu.

To create a section in your message, follow these steps:

1. Create a new mail message. Type several paragraphs in the body field.

Twistie

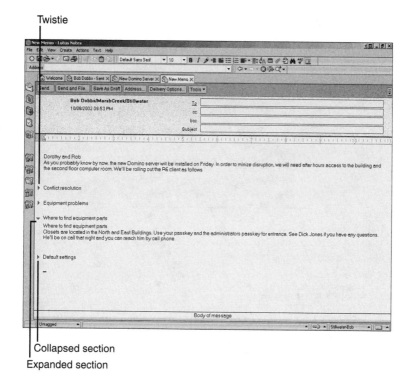

Collapsed section
Expanded section

FIGURE 16.7
Twisties are indicators that the document contains collapsed sections.

2. Select the paragraph or paragraphs you want to make into a section.

3. Choose **Create, Section** from the menu.

The first 128 characters of the paragraph become the section title. If you want to change it, follow these steps:

1. Click the section title.

2. Choose **Section, Section Properties** from the menu (see Figure 16.8).

FIGURE 16.8
In the Section properties box, set the option to create a section title, visible even when the section is collapsed.

3. Click the **Title** tab.

4. Select **Text**, and then replace the text in the Title box with the section title you want. Don't use carriage returns, hotspots, or buttons in section titles.

5. Under Section Border, choose a **Border Style** from the list box and a **Border Color** from the list box.

6. If you want to hide the title of the section when it expands, click the **Expand/Collapse** tab, and check **Hide Title When Expanded** (see Figure 16.9).

If you want to format the section title, select it and choose **Section, Section Properties**. Click the Font tab; select the font, size, style, and color you want for the section title.

You can copy and move sections as you would any other text or paragraphs with Cut, Copy, and Paste commands. For more information on rearranging text, see Lesson 15, "Editing and Formatting Text and Fields." When you want to remove a section but still want to keep all the text in the section, select the section and choose **Section, Remove**

Section from the menu. If you want to remove the section and all its text, however, choose **Edit**, **Clear** or press the **Delete** key.

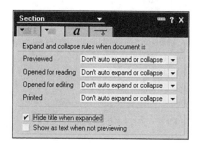

FIGURE 16.9
The Expand/Collapse tab of the Section Properties box is where you set expand and collapse options for each section.

SECTIONS AND THE INTERNET

When sending documents containing sections over the Internet, the title of the section is lost but the text in the section remains. In that case you might want the title repeated in the section text.

CREATING LINK MESSAGES

Link Messages are used to send a document link to mail correspondents. By using the Link Message feature of Notes, you also use a special mail template that fills the entire mail message in for you except for the To, cc, and bcc fields. For example, say a new policy is created in your HR Policy database, and you want to bring that to the attention of a Mail Memo recipient. Create a Link Message, and send that message to your co-worker.

To create a Link Message, follow these steps:

1. Open or select the document to which you want to create a link for your mail correspondents. The document does not need to be in your Mail database. It can be a Web page, a Notes document, or a Notes database or view.

2. Choose **Create, Mail, Special, Link Message** from the menu. A Link Message document opens (see Figure 6.10).

3. Enter the name(s) of the recipient(s) in the **To** field and change the Subject if necessary. Use the action buttons to add **Delivery Options,** and **Send** the message as you would any other mail message.

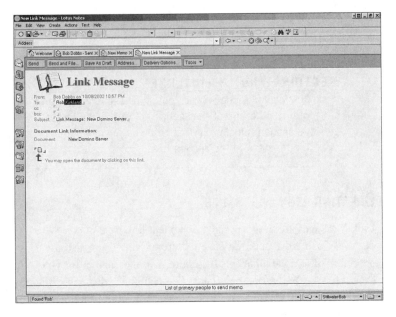

FIGURE 16.10
The Link Message automatically creates the message for you, and you only have to add the names of the recipients.

When your recipient gets the Link Message in the mail, she opens it and clicks the link icon to open the document you wanted to share with her.

ACCESS REQUIRED

Your recipient must have access to the database, Notes server, and/or Internet location that contains the document for which you sent the link. If not, she won't be able to open it. Remember, not everyone has access to your Mail database, so you are better off replying with history or forwarding mail messages instead of using Link Messages with mail documents.

In this lesson, you learned how to create links, tables, and sections. In the next lesson, you learn how to create attachments.

LESSON 17
Working with Attachments

In this lesson, you learn how to create, manage, detach, and launch file attachments.

UNDERSTANDING ATTACHMENTS

There might be times when you want to send a file to someone through email. That file might be a Domino database, a spreadsheet, a word processing document, a compressed file, a graphics file, or a scanned photograph of your grandchildren—almost any type of file. In Lotus Notes, you can attach an entire file within the rich text field, or body, of your mail message and send it. The file you attach is a copy, so your original remains intact on your computer.

The user who receives your mail can detach your file and save it. If the recipient has the same application program in which the file was created, she can launch the application, opening the file in its native application.

Attachments can be placed only in rich text fields, and the body of the mail message (where you type your message) is the only rich text field in the Mail Message form.

NOT JUST FOR MAIL

Although you tend to use attachments most often when working with your mail database, you can attach a file to any database document that has a rich text, or body, field. For example, in a personnel database there might be an attachment in a person's document that is a scanned picture—the person's portrait.

CREATING ATTACHMENTS

To attach a file to a Lotus Notes mail message, do the following:

1. Create the mail message. Make sure your insertion point (cursor) is in the message body at the exact point at which you want the attachment to appear.

2. Choose **File, Attach** or click the **File Attach** SmartIcon. The Create Attachments dialog box appears, as shown in Figure 17.1.

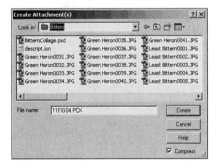

FIGURE 17.1
The Create Attachment(s) dialog box allows you to search your file system for an attachment.

3. In the Create Attachments dialog box, enter the name of the file you want to attach in the **File Name** box and then specify its location by choosing the correct drive and directory, or folder. Or, specify the location first and then select the filename from the list.

4. The **Compress** box is enabled by default. Leave this box checked.

COMPRESSED FILES

Compressed files transfer faster than those that are not compressed. It might take a little longer to attach the file to your message, however, because Notes compresses the file during the attachment process. A compressed file also takes up less disk space on the server. Don't expect the compressed file to be delivered faster over the Internet; a compressed file takes the same amount of time as an uncompressed file. If you want to send compressed files via the Internet, use a compression program such as WinZip.

5. Click the **Create** button. The attached file appears as an icon within the body of your mail message.

The appearance of the icon depends on the type of file it represents and whether you have the original software that this file was created in installed on your PC. If you are attaching a Lotus 1-2-3 file, you see a Lotus 1-2-3 icon in your mail message. If the file is a Microsoft Word file, you see a Microsoft Word icon in your mail message. If you don't have native software installed for that file, you see a generic document icon.

When you receive mail that has an attachment, a paper clip icon appears next to the mail message in your Inbox (see Figure 17.2).

TIP

You can add attachments to Notes documents by dragging and dropping them from your file system. To do this, resize your Lotus Notes program window and open and resize your My Documents folder (or the Windows Explorer window that displays the file you want to drag). Place the windows side-by-side and drag the file from My Documents to a rich text field in your Lotus Notes document or mail memo.

FIGURE 17.2
A paper clip icon in the Inbox indicates that the document has an attachment.

VIEWING ATTACHMENTS

When you receive an attached file, you can view, open, edit, save, or remove the file. Viewing a file means that you can see the file contents, even if you don't have the application in which the file was created. To view a file, open the mail message, double-click the attachment icon, and click the **View** button in the Properties box (see Figure 17.3). You might not be able to see the file exactly as it was originally formatted because the Notes Viewer doesn't read all formatting from all software programs, but the Viewer provides a menu that lets you see the file in different ways depending on the type of file. For example, you can display a spreadsheet file with or without gridlines. After you finish looking at the file, press **Esc** to leave the view.

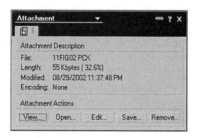

FIGURE 17.3
The Attachment Properties box provides details about the file and enables you to view, open, edit, save, or remove the attachment.

The Properties box also gives you information about the attached file: its name, the size of the file, and the date and time when it was last modified.

CAN'T VIEW OR LAUNCH AN ATTACHMENT?
There are three possible reasons for failing to view or open an attachment. First, the Attachment Viewer must be installed on your PC in order to view the attachment. If it is not, consult with your Notes Administrator. Second, the file you are trying to view must be one supported by Lotus Notes. Many types of files are supported by Lotus Notes; for a complete list, consult the **Help** database and from the **Index** view, do a quick search for **attachments**, then click **supported file formats**, and select **Opening, saving or deleting attachments** and click on **To view file attachments.** Lastly, if you're trying to *launch* the attachment, you must have access to the application that was used to create the file.

REMOVING FILES

To remove the attached file, do the following:

1. Double-click the attached file icon.

2. Click the **Remove** button on the Properties box.

3. This removes the file from your email but first gives you a warning as shown in Figure 17.4.

4. Click **Yes** to proceed and remove the attachment.

To save, remove, or save and remove more than one attachment, right-click one of the attachments and choose **Save All**, **Save and Remove All**, or **Remove All** from the pop-up menu. When you choose to save attachments, the Save Attachment dialog box appears, as shown in Figure 17.5. Specify the drive and directory, or folder, in which you want to save the files. Click **OK**.

FIGURE 17.4
The Remove Attachment dialog box warns you that removing a file cannot be undone. Removing a file from an email does not save the file to your hard drive. Instead, it deletes the file completely.

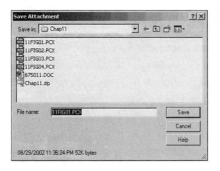

FIGURE 17.5
The Save Attachment dialog box. When you choose Save All, the title of this dialog box says "Save Attachments To:" and it will save all the attachments in your email to the folder you indicate.

OPENING FILES

If you want to look at an attached file in the application in which it was created, opening the file launches the application from within Notes mail. To open an attachment, double-click the attachment icon and then click the **Open** button on the Properties box. You can then view the document and make changes. You can save it or print it from the application. You can close the application when you finish with the file. Lotus Notes and your mail message remain open the entire time you are working in the other applications.

OUT FOR LAUNCH

If you can't launch the attachment, you probably don't have that application installed on your computer. You can still use the View option, as described in the beginning of this lesson, to see the unformatted contents of the attachment.

EDITING THE ATTACHMENT

This is a new feature in Lotus Notes 6 and one we really appreciate, as we feel it's one of the most useful end-user features in 6. Editing an attachment allows you to open the attachment in its originating software, and when you save your changes, Notes automatically saves your changes in the attachment. For example, in previous versions of Notes, if you received an email with a Word document and a request to make changes or edits to that document, you had to open the document in Word, make changes, save the document to your hard drive, create a new mail memo, and send the changes back to the sender. In 6, you simply choose **Edit** in the attachment properties box, edit the document in Word, click **Save**, and close Word, and you are automatically returned to the email in Lotus Notes. Press the **Esc** key and Notes will ask you if you want to save your changes. Click **Save**. Now you can reply with attachments to that email, and your edited attachment will be returned to the recipient.

If you edit documents and return the edited copy to the sender, it's a good idea to save the document with a different file name. For example, if you receive PressRelease1.doc for your review and you open and edit the document, save it as PressRelease1R.doc so everyone knows that the document has been edited and is different than the document you originally received.

If you decide to make changes to a file you launched and you want to save two versions, the one you received and the one you made changes to, use the Save As command to give it a name you will remember. At the same time, specify a location on your computer where you want to store the file. Saving changes this way does not affect the original attachment sent to you.

Printing an Attachment

The easiest way to print an attachment is to open it in its originating software. If, however, you don't have the originating software installed, complete the following steps:

1. Double-click the attachment icon to open the file.

2. Click the **View** button on the Properties box.

3. Choose **File, Print**. The File Print dialog box appears. The default setting in the File Print dialog box is to print all of the document. If you want to print only a portion of the attachment, highlight that segment before you choose **File, Print**. Then, after you open the File Print dialog box, choose **Selection** under Print Range. For more information on printing, see Lesson 4, "Managing Mail."

4. Click **OK** to print the document.

Unexpected results, such as code lines or unusual characters, might occur when you print from the viewer. Whenever possible, therefore, it is better to print from the native application.

In this lesson, you learned how to create, launch, edit, detach, and print attachments. In the next lesson, you learn about working with a discussion group and communicating via a discussion database. You also learn how to work in a collaborative database environment.

LESSON 18

Understanding Replication

In this lesson, you'll learn about replication, how to create a new Mail replica, and how to copy from the Public Address Book.

HOW REPLICATION WORKS

Domino servers store many databases, and when you are in the office connected to the Domino network, you can open databases on the server directly from your workstation. Most of the databases that you access, including your mail database, are stored on your home server. Often, companies have multiple Domino servers, and you need to access databases on several Domino servers in your company.

PLAIN ENGLISH

Home Server

The term used for the Domino server on which your mail database resides. If you can access several Domino servers at work, the one containing your mail database is the one referred to as your *home* server.

When you're not in the office, you need to access the server via a modem or Internet connection. If you use a modem and have a lot of work to do in a database (such as reading and replying to mail), remaining on the phone line can be costly. You'll also find that working via modem is much slower than being on the network in the office. When this situation occurs, you'll want to replicate databases.

Replication is the process of "synchronizing" the same database on different computers. It is actually a special copying process. Replication does not overwrite the entire database, as copying a database would in your file system. Instead, it updates only the documents you modified, and it does the same thing for everyone else who replicates the database. As people call in to replicate a database, they receive the most recent copy of the documents in the database on their own computers. The server receives their changes, and the server sends them any updates that have occurred since they last replicated. Eventually, the modifications circulate to everyone using the database.

When you are ready to replicate a database, you'll place a call from your computer to the server in your office. After the two computers "shake hands" and recognize each other, your computer begins sending updates you made to the database replicas. Then your computer receives any modifications made to the database since you last replicated. The replication process is illustrated in Figure 18.1.

Now look at replication with regard to your Mail database. To receive your mail, you call in to the server from home (or from the road) and replicate your Mail database. After you disconnect from the server, you read your mail, reply to some messages, delete some messages, and file some messages in folders. During this time, Mary Jones creates a new mail message for you, which is waiting on the server replica of your mail database. When you finish reading and replying to mail, you call in to the server and replicate mail again. During this replication period, the changes you made while disconnected (new replies, deletions, and so forth) are sent to the server copy of your mail database, and Mary's new message is sent to your replica of the database.

Each database has a unique *replica ID* that identifies it as a genuine replica and not just a copy of the database (see Figure 18.2). If the database on your computer does not have the same ID as the one on the server, replication won't occur.

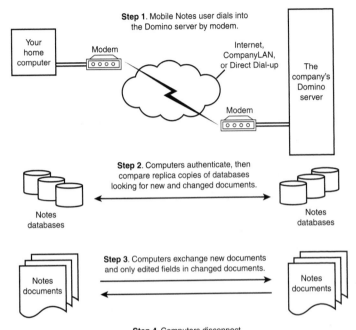

Step 1. Mobile Notes user dials into the Domino server by modem.

Your home computer

Modem

Internet, CompanyLAN, or Direct Dial-up

The company's Domino server

Modem

Step 2. Computers authenticate, then compare replica copies of databases looking for new and changed documents.

Notes databases

Notes databases

Step 3. Computers exchange new documents and only edited fields in changed documents.

Notes documents

Notes documents

Step 4. Computers disconnect.

FIGURE 18.1

Every time you replicate, changes made to the database since your last replication are added to your replica copy.

FIGURE 18.2

The Database Properties box displays the Replica ID on the Info tab.

Before replicating, the server also checks to see when the replica copy of the database on your computer was last modified. If that date is more recent than the date the database was last successfully replicated, the database replicates. The server also looks at the modification and replication dates on the server replica. If that replica was modified since the last replication, replication occurs. Domino maintains a replication history of each database you replicate (see Figure 18.3).

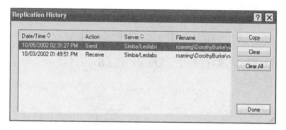

FIGURE 18.3
The Replication History displays in the dialog box and can be sorted by Date (shown) or by Server name.

When the database replicates, it updates only those document fields that have been changed since the last replication, and adds any new documents. Each document has its own *unique Notes identification number* assigned to it when it is first saved (see Figure 18.4). Part of that number is a document-level sequence number that increases each time you modify the document. If the number is higher for a particular document than the database on the server, it is replicated to the server. Any documents that you deleted or that were deleted from the server replica leave a *deletion stub*, and that is replicated so the document is deleted from other replicas of the database unless **Do not send deletions** was checked in the replication settings.

When replication is complete, you disconnect. You now have an updated copy of the database on your PC.

FIGURE 18.4
The Document Properties box displays the unique Notes identification number on the Document IDs page.

SETTING REPLICATION PREFERENCES

You can control the replication process by specifying what type of files you want to receive, how old the files can be, and the priority of the database replication. All this is controlled under Replication Settings. There are three ways to open the Replication Settings dialog box for the database you have open or selected:

- Choose **File**, **Replication**, **Settings** from the menu.

- Right-click the bookmark and select **Replication, Settings** from the shortcut menu.

- Click the **Replication Settings** button on the Database Properties box.

The Replication Settings dialog box (see Figure 18.5) has five pages of settings—Basics, Space Savers, Send, Other, and Advanced. You click the appropriate icon to change pages.

On the Basics page, you enable a replication schedule, decide how much of the database you want replicated, and select a preferred server for replication. The purpose of the options on the Space Savers page is to limit the amount of space the replica takes up on your hard disk. The Send page includes options about what types of items you want to send when replicating with the server. On the Other page, you can disable replication temporarily, specify the priority of the replication, and enter the CD-ROM publishing date. The Advanced page has options to control how you replicate with a specified server (which is important if you replicate with more than one). Table 18.1 quickly summarizes the important features of the dialog box that you might need to use.

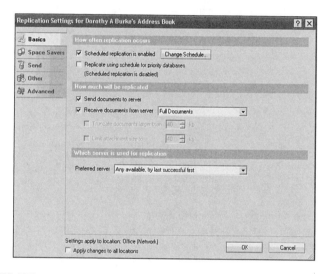

FIGURE 18.5
Replication Settings dialog box (Space Savers page) for a mail database contains options for removing old documents.

CAUTION

Check with your Domino Administrator before you begin changing replication settings or try to create a mail replica. The Administrator may have set that up for you when your Notes client was installed. If not, the Administrator may want to walk you through the steps or do it for you.

TABLE 18.1   Important Replication Settings Options

When You Need To	Set This Option (On This Page)	Description
Delete documents on your replica without deleting them on the server copy	Do not send deletions made in this replica to other replicas (Send page)	Normally, when you delete a document in your replica, a deletion stub is replicated to the server, which replicates it to all the replica copies, so your deletions affect everyone else's replica.
Eliminate documents created before a certain date	Only replicate incoming documents saved or modified after (Other page)	Specify the beginning date.
Limit the number of large attachments or memos you receive	Receive partial documents or the summary only and limit attachment size (Basics page)	Only receive the beginning of the mail memo (To, From Subject) or specify how much of the docu- ment and attach- ments you receive.
Remove old documents	Remove documents not modified in the last [specified number] days (Space Savers page)	Enter how old (in days) a document is when it's dropped from your replica.
Receive only part	Replicate a subset of documents (Space Savers page)	Check this item and then select the views and folders you want to replicate of the database (hold down Ctrl to click more than one).

TABLE 18.1   (continued)

When You Need To	Set This Option (On This Page)	Description
Stop replication	Temporarily disable replication (Other page)	If you are stopping replication because of a problem with the database, call your system administrator for assistance.

CREATING A NEW MAIL REPLICA

People who use their computers outside the office and away from the network are referred to as *mobile users*. If you're one of these mobile users, it's a good idea to replicate the important databases you need to your laptop *before* you take the laptop out of the office. This will save you time on the telephone lines (if you use a modem). Of course, the most important of the databases you want to replicate is your mail database. Before you begin, confirm with your Domino Administrator that you need to make a new Mail database replica. There could be a copy on your laptop that doesn't have a bookmark associated with it. To find out if a replica is on your computer, right-click the bookmark for your mail file and choose **Open Replica**. If **local** appears in the list of replicas, you already have the replica on your laptop. Notes is smart enough to place local replica information on the bookmark when you have opened the server copy, if the local replica exists.

Making a new replica is a straightforward process. Later in this lesson, the section "Using the Replicator Page" shows you how to update this replica (or replicate) on an ongoing basis. It's very important to make a new replica of a database only once:

1. Open your mail database, and then choose **File**, **Replication**, **New Replica** from the menu (or right-click the bookmark, and choose **Replication**, **New Replica** from the menu.

2. The **Create Replica for Database [your name]** dialog box appears (see Figure 18.6).

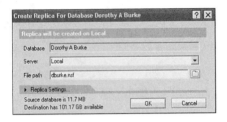

FIGURE 18.6
Click the twistie by Replica Settings to encrypt the replica, create a full text index for searching, or have the replica created immediately.

3. Make sure the Server displayed is **Local**. Notes automatically fills in the Database and the File path (you can change the path to put the file in a different location if you want).

4. Click the twistie by Replica Settings, and then select **Create Immediately**.

5. Click **OK**.

After this, any time you want to replicate (update) your mail, use the Replicator page, as shown below.

USING THE REPLICATOR PAGE

The Replicator page provides a central location to handle all your replication needs. By using the features available on the Replicator page (see Figure 18.7), you can set options to control which databases replicate and with which servers you are replicating. To open the Replicator page, click the Replication bookmark on the Bookmark bar.

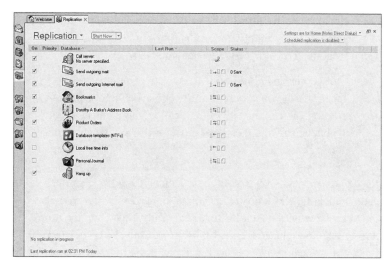

FIGURE 18.7
The Replicator page contains Call Server and Hang up entries if the current location uses direct dialup to connect to a Notes server.

There are several rows, or entries, on the Replicator page:

- **Send outgoing mail** and **Send outgoing Internet mail**—
  Sends all pending messages from your Outgoing Mail databases. These databases hold your outgoing mail when you
  work offline. When you use the Replicator page, the outgoing
  mail gets routed to the server.

- **Databases**—For each local database replica that you have,
  there is a database entry on the Replicator page.

- **Database templates**—Templates are used to create new databases and to refresh the designs of any template-based databases you have. You probably will not need to replicate your
  templates with the server. (You need to do this only to update
  your templates.)

- **Local free time info**—This entry sends information from your Calendar about your availability so others who are scheduling meetings know when you are free.

- **Call server** and **Hang up**—These entries automatically appear when you choose the Home (Notes Direct Dialup) location. When you activate replication, these entries place the phone call and then hang up automatically when replication is completed.

Each entry row also has a check box. To include an entry in the replication, click the check box (a check mark appears). When you click the **Start Now** button (select **Start Mail Only Now** from the drop-down menu to replicate the mail files only), Lotus Notes performs the functions of each checked entry row in the order of the rows.

The status bar at the bottom of the page shows information about the current replication, letting you know when Lotus Notes is attempting to call a server, what database is being replicated, the progress of the replication, how many minutes are left, and when the replication is finished. After replication, the status bar displays statistics for individual entries.

In this lesson, you learned about replication, making a new Mail replica, and using the Replicator page. In the next lesson, you learn how to use Notes remotely.

LESSON 19
Using Notes Remotely

In this lesson, you'll learn how to work with Notes when you aren't in the office—by replicating mail, creating replicas of databases, and encrypting local databases.

UNDERSTANDING NOTES MOBILE USERS

A *mobile* user is one who works in Notes while disconnected from the Notes network. You become a mobile user when you are working at a desktop computer from home or by using a laptop computer from a client site, a regional office, home, or hotel. As a mobile user, you connect to the Notes network via a modem and a phone line (if you have a cable or DSL line at home, you can probably connect as if you were in the office) .

Before you leave the office to go on the road, make sure of the following:

- Your location and connection documents are set up.

- Your replicas are created, and you've added any necessary entries to the Replicator page.

- You have a phone cord, extra battery packs, and a power adapter.

- You have the phone number for your Domino Administrator. (Please don't tell him we suggested you travel with his cell phone number, home phone number, and beeper number!)

- You have a copy of the Help database on your computer.

There are two ways to connect to the Domino server using a modem and a phone line.

- **Network Dialup connection**—This type of connection lets you call into a single network server. Once you connect to that server, you have access to all the Domino servers in your organization and possibly the Internet. Although you are using a slower connection, it's almost like being on the Local Area Network (LAN) in the office.

- **Notes Direct Dialup**—With this type of connection, you dial directly into a Domino server.

You don't want to read and reply to mail while connected to the server over a modem. Working while connected via a modem is time-consuming and possibly expensive, particularly if you are calling long distance. Therefore, mobile users generally replicate their mail databases to their laptops or desktops at home. You can work in your local replica, saving phone time for the replication process. By doing this, you can access your data quickly, make and store all new documents and updates, and send everything back to the server in one short phone call (see Lesson 18, "Understanding Replication," for more information on the replication process).

 TIP

Depending on how your organization sets up its Web access, it's possible to access your mail or other database with a Web browser with no need to install the Notes client on your laptop. Check with your Domino Administrator to find out if you can do this. Also, read Appendix A, "Understanding Security and Access Rights," under the section "Web Access to Mail" before you contact your Administrator.

Setting Up to Connect

If your Domino Administrator does not set up your computer for you so you can remotely access the server, you will have to do some work to prepare Notes to connect using a phone line and modem, especially if you were not using the modem when Notes was installed on your computer.

First, you need to gather some information:

- The name of your home server (the server where your mail file is stored).

- The phone number, including area code, you need to dial to connect to your network server (if you are using network dialup) or your home server.

- The type of modem you have (look in the operating system's Control Panel under Phone and Modem, if you don't know).

- The name of the COM port to which your modem is connected (also found in the Control Panel under Phone and Modem).

Start by switching to the Location document you need to configure. A Location document contains such details as how to connect to your network, where to find your mail database, how to dial the phone, and what port to use. Six location documents automatically appear during the installation process: Home (Network Dialup), Home (Notes Direct Dialup), Internet, Island (Disconnected), Office (Network), and Travel (Notes Direct Dialup). To switch to the location you need, click the **Location** button on the Status bar and then click on the location name in the pop-up menu—either Home (Network Dialup) or Home (Notes Direct Dialup).

To configure the Location you chose, do the following:

1. Choose **File, Preferences, Client Reconfiguration Wizard**
   from the menu to open Lotus Notes Client Configuration dialog box (see Figure 19.1). By answering the questions in this
   wizard and selecting options, you automatically configure
   both your Location document and a server connection document (it contains information on what it takes to connect to
   the server, such as its phone number).

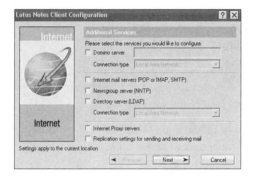

FIGURE 19.1
Select Domino server and then choose a Connection type.

2. In the dialog box, select **Domino server** and then enter the
   name of your home server.

3. Select a Connection type, such as **Network Dialup** or **Notes
   Direct Dialup**. Choose **Passthru server** only if the server
   you must dial in to is not your home server; it is an interme-
   diary server that allows you connect to the home server.

4. Enable the other options only if you know you need them,
   such as an Internet mail server. Check with your Domino
   Administrator first if you don't know.

5. Click **Next**. Enter the phone number of the Domino server,
   including area code. If you have to dial a prefix, such as 8 or
   9, in order to get an outside line, enter that in the Dialing
   Prefix box.

6. Click **Next**. Select your modem type. If it isn't in the list, select **AutoConfigure**.

7. Click **Next**. Select your modem port.

8. Click **Next**. The dialog box closes. Your configuration is complete.

NOTE

When you are on the road, use the Travel (Notes Direct Dialup) location if you need to connect via direct dialup. It sets up the same way as the Home (Notes Direct Dialup). When you switch to the Travel location, a dialog box appears asking about how you dial out from your present location (using a prefix or country code) and what your local time, date, and time zone are.

CREATING REPLICAS REMOTELY

When you need to work on databases that are stored on the server at the office, but you're working away from the office, it's always best to create replicas while you are still in the office. But if that's not possible, you can do it when you connect via modem (it's just slower).

NETWORK DIALUP

The instructions for calling in and creating a new replica from the server do not apply to you if you use Network Dialup instead of dialing in directly to your Domino server. You should use the instructions in Lesson 18 under the section "Creating a New Mail Replica" to create your new replicas.

To start the process of creating a new replica, you need to call the server (your administrator can tell you which one):

1. Choose **File, Mobile, Call Server** from the menu. The Call
   Server dialog box appears (see Figure 19.2) .

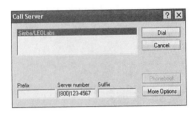

FIGURE 19.2
If you call in to more than one server, all servers are listed in the Call Server dialog box, and you select the one you want to call.

2. Pick the name of the server you want to call (if you have
   more than one).

3. Click **Dial**. The status bar indicates when you are connected.

The first time you connect, you need to make the replica copy of the
database. After that, you use the Replicator page (see Lesson 18) to
replicate modifications and new documents with the server. It's very
important to make a new replica of a database only once:

1. Choose **File, Database, Open** from the menu. When the
   Open Database dialog box appears (see Figure 19.3), select
   the name of the server from the Server drop-down list.

2. From the Database list, select the database you want and then
   click **Open**.

3. After the database opens, choose **File, Replication, New
   Replica**.

   In the Create Replica for Database [database name] dialog
   box (see Figure 19.4), make sure the Server displayed is
   Local. Notes automatically fills in the **Database** and the **File
   Path**.

FIGURE 19.3
The Open Database dialog box.

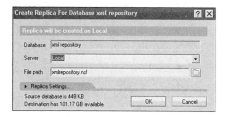

FIGURE 19.4
The Create Replica for Database dialog box.

4. Click the twistie to expand Replica Settings and then select **Create Immediately**.

5. Click **OK**.

Repeat the set of instructions above for each database for which you need a new replica. When your call is complete, you need to disconnect from the server.

1. Choose **File, Mobile, Hang Up** from the menu.

2. When a dialog box appears with your modem port highlighted, click **Hang Up**.

USING OUTGOING MAIL

When you work with a replica of the mail database, outgoing mail is stored temporarily in the Outgoing Mailbox database. The outgoing mail is sent when you replicate or send mail to the server, and the Outgoing Mailbox database mailbox is emptied. Incoming mail is automatically deposited in your Inbox.

To see the mail that is waiting to be sent, open the Outgoing Mail database by choosing **File, Database, Open** from the menu. You won't see the Outgoing Mail database listed in the databases. You need to enter the name in the Filename box or select it by clicking the **Browse** button. Look for the mail.box file in your \Notes\Data directory (you'll have to change the Files of type setting to All Files). Select the file and click **Select**. Click **Open** to see the database. You might want to bookmark the database if you intend to use it again.

You can view a list of the messages awaiting delivery, but you can't read the mail message from the Outgoing Mail database.

GETTING YOUR MEMO BACK

When you're connected to a LAN or WAN, you can't snatch your mail back after you've sent it. Deleting the Mail Memo from your mail database won't stop its delivery. When you work remotely, however, you can stop the mail before it gets to the server. If you haven't replicated or sent mail yet, the mail is still in the Outgoing Mail database. Open the database, select the mail message, and click the **Delete Message** button on the Action bar. You'll also have to delete your copy of it in your mail database.

REPLICATING MAIL

Access the Replicator page by clicking the Replication bookmark. The Replicator page provides a central location to handle all your replication needs. By using the features available on the Replicator page, you can set options to control replication of your mail and any other databases you might use. Lotus Notes automatically creates a **Send Outgoing Mail** entry on the Replicator page, as shown in Figure 19.5. For information on how Replicator page works, see "Using the Replicator Page" in Lesson 18.

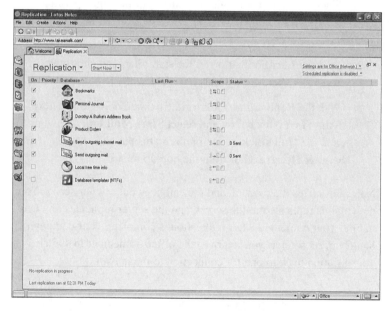

FIGURE 19.5
The Replicator Page.

There may also be entries for your mail database (if you have a local replica) and for sending outgoing Internet mail. To replicate, click

Start Now. To replicate only the mail files, click the arrow next to Start Now and select **Start Mail Only Now.**

At the bottom of the Replicator page, you'll see the progress of the replication. After replication is complete, a note appears at the bottom of the page indicating when the last replication was completed.

USING SEND/RECEIVE MAIL

To send and receive mail while working remotely, follow these steps:

1. Plug one end of the phone cord into your modem's port and the other into a phone jack on the wall or on the back of a phone.

2. Click the **Location** button on the status bar, and choose your current location if it's not already selected.

3. Click the **Replication** bookmark. Click the down arrow next to the **Start Now** button and select **Start Mail Only Now,** or click the **Quickpick** button on the status bar and choose **Send & Receive Mail** from the pop-up menu.

Notes initializes the modem, and the call goes out to your server. Your new mail is replicated to the server, and the server replicates any new mail to your computer. After replication is complete, your computer hangs up. As soon as you return to the office, remember to switch your location back to one for connection to the network.

MY OTHER DATABASES DIDN'T REPLICATE!

Sending and receiving mail does not replicate your other databases—only your mail database. You must click the **Start Now** button on the Replicator page to replicate other databases. To replicate some, but not all, select the database(s) you want before you click **Start Now.**

ENCRYPTING LOCAL DATABASES

Security is an issue in every company, and should your laptop become lost or stolen, the information stored in your Notes databases is no longer secure. To help ensure that information on your laptop is available to only you, encrypt the local copies of databases on your laptop.

ENCRYPTION CAN SLOW YOU DOWN!
Encrypted databases can take a long time to open. Use encryption only if you have a real security issue.

To encrypt a local copy of a database, follow these steps:

1. Right-click the database bookmark, and choose **Database, Properties**.

2. On the Database Basics tab, click the **Encryption Settings** button.

3. From the **Locally Encrypt This Database Using** drop-down list (see Figure 19.6), select **Medium** encryption. Select **Strong** encryption only if your system administrator instructs you to do so.

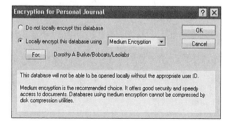

FIGURE 19.6
Choose to locally encrypt databases in the Encryption dialog box.

4. Click **OK**.

WORKING OFFLINE

Although it's horrible to contemplate, there are times when you won't be able to connect to the server—via a LAN, a WAN, or a modem. For example, you might be traveling by plane or train or staying in an older hotel/motel with hard-wired phones. In these cases, you can only work *offline*. Change your location to **Island (Disconnected)** so your computer does not attempt to connect to the server if you accidentally try to open one of the databases only found on the server.

Remember to change your location when you reach a site where you can connect to the server.

In this lesson, you learned how to work remotely with Notes. In the next lesson, you learn how to customize and set preferences in Notes.

Lesson 20
Customizing Notes

In this lesson, you learn how to customize the way you work in Notes through the use of user preferences. You also learn about customizing toolbars.

Setting User Preferences

You can change a number of settings that affect your workspace and how you work in Notes, such as when Notes scans for unread documents, when your trash is emptied, and whether Notes saves a copy of the mail you send. Find these settings and options in the **User Preferences** dialog box (shown in Figure 20.1). To open the **User Preferences** dialog box, choose **File**, **Preferences**, **User Preferences**.

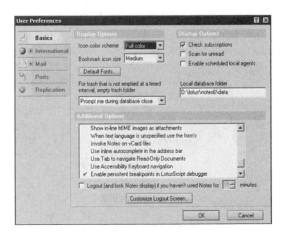

FIGURE 20.1
*Keep in mind that some of the Preference settings won't take effect until the next time that you start Notes. Usually, you'll see an alert to that effect after you click **OK**.*

PLAIN ENGLISH

More Information

This lesson covers only the common, most basic options you can customize in **User Preferences**. If you need more information about customizing **User Preferences**, see *the Special Edition Using Lotus Noes and Domino 6.*

In the User Preferences dialog box, you can change your preferences in five areas: Basics, International, Mail, Ports, and Replication. The dialog box opens with the Basics section highlighted (refer to Figure 20.1). Table 20.1 describes areas where you might want to make changes. For items you find in the properties box that are not covered here, please consult with your System Administrator.

TABLE 20.1   User Preferences Basics Options

Option	Description
Display options	You choose your icon color scheme, bookmark size, and default font in this section. Use the drop-down menus.
Startup options	Contains check boxes for commands that are performed automatically when you open Notes. Place a check mark in the **Scan for unread** check box if you want Notes to look for unread messages and documents. Put a check mark in the **Prompt for location** box if you are a mobile user or if more than one person shares a workstation (See Lesson 19, "Using Notes Remotely"). If you are set up to use subscriptions, select the **Check Subscriptions** check box to display new additions when you open Notes.
Lock ID file	A security measure that prompts you to type in your password if Notes has been inactive for a designated number of minutes.

TABLE 20.1   User Preferences Basics Options

Option	Description
	For trash that is not emptied at a timed interval, empty trash folderGoverns when your trash folder is emptied. Choose whether you want to be prompted when you close the database, whether you always want it emptied when you close the database, or whether you want to empty it manually. (To learn more about using the trash folder, see Lesson 4, "Managing Mail.")
Additional options	Contains a list of options that control how you use Notes. A check mark appears beside active options. Click an option to select or deselect it. Use the scrollbar on the right of this window to see all available options.
Security Options	Displays Workstation Execution Control Lists. You should not modify any of these options unless you are instructed to do so by your Domino System Administrator.

UNSURE OF THE ADDITIONAL OPTIONS?
If you're unsure of an option's meaning, read about the option in Notes Help system before you activate it. Also, check with your System Administrator or Notes Help Desk before you make advanced settings if you are unsure of the results. If you do check an option and you don't like the results, open the **User Preferences** dialog box and deselect it.

Most of the International settings are determined at the time when the Domino server or the workstation is set up. For the most part, you will leave the settings as they are pictured in Figure 20.2. Table 20.2 high-lights some of those options. Click the **+** sign next to International to reveal three subsections: General, Spell Check, and Calendar.

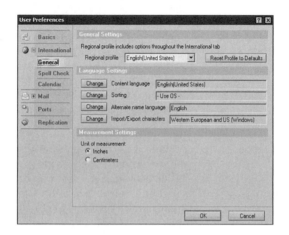

FIGURE 20.2
Most International Options never need changing as they are set when Notes is installed on your workstation.

TABLE 20.2   International Options

Option	Description
General	Select the default language settings for Notes.
Spell Check	Select your dictionary (language), and when you need to edit your personal dictionary, click **Edit User Dictionary**. Editing the user dictionary enables you to view words you've added to your User Dictionary during spell checking. You can add, update, and delete any of these words. (For more information on using Spell Check, see Lesson 3, "Creating and Sending Mail.") You can also install specialized language dictionaries here.

TABLE 20.2   (continued)

Option	Description
Calendar	By default, the Calendar View starts on Monday as seen in Lesson 9, "Using the Calendar." You can select a different day of the week if your work week does not begin on Monday. You can also set defaults for the date picker here.

As seen in Figure 20.3, you can change Mail options by clicking the **Mail** icon in the **User Preferences** dialog box, which opens two subsections: **General** and **Internet**. Table 20.3 describes some of the mail options you might want to change.

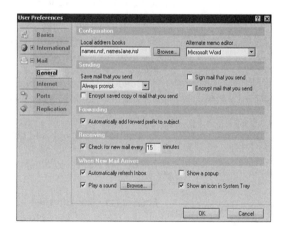

FIGURE 20.3
*Mail options are changed in this section of the **User Preferences** dialog box.*

TABLE 20.3   Mail Options

Option	Description
General—Configuration	**Local Address Books**—By default, Notes uses your local address book, called "names.nsf". You can add more that one address book so Notes uses two or more address books, but

TABLE 20.3   (continued)

Option	Description
	this requires you to name the address books differently, for example, "names.nsf", "names2.nsf", and so forth. For more information on how to do this, search the Help database for "local address books".
	Alternate memo editor—This advanced Mail feature enables you to use either Microsoft Word or Lotus WordPro for creating mail messages. In order for this to work, you must have the software installed on your workstation.
General—Sending	**Save mail that you send**—Controls whether Notes always keeps a copy of the mail messages you send, never keeps a copy, or prompts you so you can decide at the time you send the message whether to keep a copy of the message.
	Encrypt saved copy of mail that you send—Tells Notes to always protect the mail you save so others cannot view it.
	Encrypt mail that you send—Encrypts all the messages that you send.
	Sign mail that you send—Tells Notes to always add a digital signature to your mail.
General—Forwarding	**Automatically add forward prefix to subject**—Fills in the subject line using text from the original memo preceded by "Fw".
General—Receiving	**Check for new mail every (fill in) minutes**—The default value for checking for new mail while connected to the server is 15 minutes. Change this value if you need to.

TABLE 20.3   (continued)

Option	Description
General—When new mail arrives	**Automatically Refresh Inbox**—Choose this option so Notes displays new messages in your Inbox upon receipt. If you deselect this option, a refresh icon will appear in the header of your Inbox and you'll need to click the Refresh button or press F9 to display new messages.
	Play a sound—Controls whether Notes sounds a beep or any other sound upon receipt of new mail. You can select a different notification sound by clicking on the **Browse** button and then selecting the sound from the list. Notes or Notes Minder must be running for audible notification to work.
	Show a popup—Choose this option so Notes displays a pop-up message on your screen when you receive new mail. Notes or Notes Minder must be running for visible notification to work.
	Show an icon in system Tray—Choose this message to have Notes notify you of new mail by placing an icon in your Windows system tray. Notes or Notes Minder must be running for visible notification to work.
Internet	Internet options control the behavior of mail with regard to sending mail through the Internet. Consult the Help database or your System Administrator before you change settings in this section.

The **Ports** options determine how your workstation connects to the Domino server. Do not change these setting unless you are instructed to do so by your Domino System Administrator.

The Replication section of the User Preferences dialog box controls how Notes behaves during replication. Some of these options are discussed in Lesson 18, "Understanding Replication," and Lesson 19 "Using Notes Remotely."

When you finish changing settings in the **User Preferences** dialog box, click **OK** to close it.

SETTING TOOLBAR PREFERENCES

Most Windows products contain a toolbar with icons that act as shortcuts or alternatives to using the menu. Some people find it faster to click an icon on the toolbar than to look through the menus to find choices such as opening a database or bolding text. Like menus and Action bars, toolbars are *context-sensitive* by default; that is, they change as the tasks you perform in Notes change.

SEMPER FIDELIS

The first six icons to the right of the first spacer are always available. They will not change as you move from task to task in Notes.

To help you understand the function of each icon, Lotus Notes has a feature that shows the icons' descriptions. To see this brief description, hold your mouse over an icon. If the description does not appear, you might need to turn this feature on. Here's how to turn on the icon descriptions:

1. From your workspace, open the **File** menu and click **Preferences** and then **Toolbar Preferences**. The **Toolbar Preferences** dialog box appears, as shown in Figure 20.4.

2. Click the **Basics** button and in the **Toolbar Appearance** section, select **Show pop up description text** to display descriptions.

3. Click **OK**.

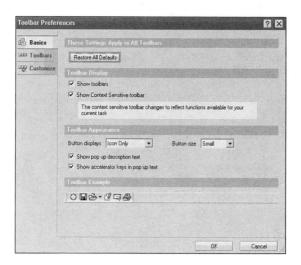

FIGURE 20.4
In the Toolbar Preferences box, you can change the way icons appear on your toolbar by changing the Button displays to "icon only", "text only", or "icon and text". You can also change the size of icons in the Button size field.

To see or change the available toolbars, click the **Toolbars** icon on the Toolbar Preferences box. Select the toolbars you want displayed by placing a check mark next to the toolbar name.

To customize or modify a toolbar, click the **Customize** button in the Toolbar Preferences dialog box and follow these steps:

1. Select the toolbar you wish to modify in the **Select the Toolbar to modify** drop-down field (see Figure 20.5).

2. In the **Available Buttons** list, click on the icon you wish to add or remove and click either the **Add Button** or **Remove** button. Do this for each icon you wish to change on the toolbar.

3. (Optional)The icons (buttons) displayed in the box are sorted by function. If you want to see them in order of description, click the **Sort Buttons** button and choose **by description**.

4. As you add or remove icons, they appear in the **Toolbar Contents** section along with the all other icons contained in that toolbar. To change the order of the icons in the toolbar, highlight the icon you wish to move and click the **Left** or **Right** buttons in the Reorder section.

5. When you're finished, click **Save Toolbar** or **Restore Defaults** and then click **OK** to close the dialog box.

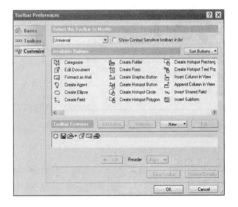

FIGURE 20.5
You can modify toolbars and add new buttons in the Customize tab of the Toolbar Preferences dialog box

You can float a toolbar in Notes (see Figure 20.6). A floating toolbar appears in its own window rather than being anchored on the edge of the screen (as in Right, Left, Top, or Bottom). To float a toolbar, place your mouse on the separator bar and drag the toolbar to the area of the screen you desire.

Click the Separator bar to drag

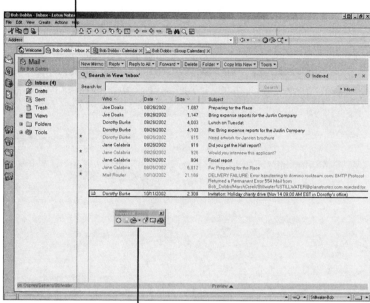

Floating toolbar

FIGURE 20.6
Float toolbars in your work area by dragging them to a desired position. To return a toolbar to its original position, click and drag it to that position and release the mouse button.

CUSTOMIZING THE WELCOME PAGE

You can customize the appearance of your Welcome page. Options for customizing the Welcome page are

- Choose from a list of available styles
- Customize an available style by changing its template

- Create your own page
- Use a bookmark as your Welcome page
- Customize a Welcome page background or contents

To create your own page or customize a Welcome page style, open the customize area by clicking the arrow next to **Click here for Welcome Page options** on your Welcome page (See Figure 20.7).

Click the triangle to open or close the Welcome Page options

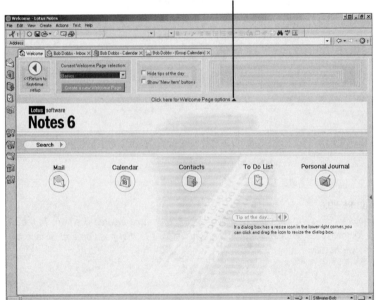

FIGURE 20.7
Customize, change, edit, or create a new Welcome page by opening the Welcome Page Options.

In the **Current Welcome Page Selection** field, use the drop-down menu to select a style for your Welcome page. The default selection for this page, unless changed by your Administrator, is the **Basics** page (shown in Figure 20.7). Choose **Headlines with My Lycos**,

Headlines with my UK Lycos or **Headlines with Terra** for a
Welcome page that includes the Lycos or Terra home pages. **Basics
Plus** displays a Welcome page that includes Notes search options,
your Calendar, To Do list, and Inbox (see Figure 20.8).

CAUTION

No templates? No options? Your Welcome page is customizable by your Notes Administrator. It's entirely possible that a corporate Welcome page has been designed
for your use and you may find that options mentioned
here do not apply to your Notes desktop.

FIGURE 20.8
*The Basics Plus Welcome Page displays many areas of Notes, including your
Calendar and To Do list.*

When you choose **My Page** from the drop-down list, you have the
opportunity to customize the page. To create a brand new page, click

the **Create a new Welcome Page** button located under the **Current Welcome Page selection** field. When you create a new Welcome page (see Figure 20.9), the New Page Wizard walks you through the design of your new page.

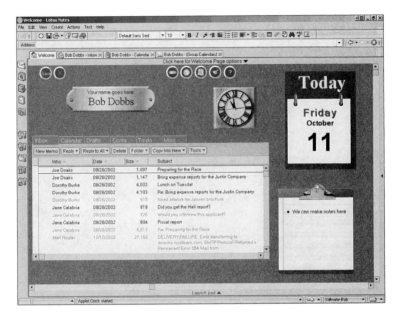

FIGURE 20.9

Using the New Page Wizard and using layout "f" from the Welcome page gallery, we created this new customized Welcome page. The clipboard tablet allows us to make notes on our Welcome page, which we can edit or change at any time by clicking the Edit button on the Welcome page.

In this lesson, you learned how to customize user preferences, change your Welcome page, and customize toolbars.

Appendix A

Understanding Security and Access Rights

Notes security is a powerful, important tool for your company. Lotus Notes and Domino security has several levels of access. Notes administrators and designers can determine the following:

- Who can access the server
- Who can access each database
- Who can access views and documents within a database
- Who can access fields within a form

Ability to access the server is determined by your Notes ID and password. Whether you can access a database and what you can do within the database is determined by the Access Control List (ACL) for each database.

Passwords

Your first line of defense in securing your system and mail from unauthorized people is your password. When you access the Domino server the first time, you start a Notes session, which prompts you to enter your password. For security reasons, neither you nor anyone else can see what you are typing—all you see are X's.

Your password can be any combination of keyboard characters, as long as the first character is a letter of the alphabet. The minimum number of characters in your password is determined when your Notes ID (User ID) is created by your Domino Administrator. Because passwords are case-sensitive, the password "INFONUT" is different from the password "infonut".

The User ID is a file created when the Domino Administrator first registers you as a user. When you start up Lotus Notes on your computer for the first time, the User ID file transfers to your computer and by default is placed in the Lotus\Notes\Data directory or folder. It might be called user.id or a shortened version of your name plus the .id extension. You want to be careful to protect this file, because someone else could use it to pretend to be you on the Lotus Notes network. If your computer's operating system is password-protected, that might be enough. If your computer is accessible to several people, however, or if you share a computer at work, you might want to move the User ID file off of your computer onto a floppy disk for safekeeping. If you ever suspect the file is lost (along with your stolen laptop), report it to the Notes administrator.

Lotus Notes has several features designed to limit access to documents, views, databases, and servers. For example, only authorized personnel can delete databases from the server, design applications, open certain documents, or read designated fields. The Domino Administrator or the Application Designer controls most of this. What you are authorized to do depends on your status in the Access Control List of each database, and that level of access won't necessarily be the same for each database you use.

A database that contains all of your company's customers might be accessible to everyone in the company, but it's very possible that different people see different views, forms, and fields, and can see only a partial list of customers. Perhaps each salesperson can see only the customers assigned to him or her when he or she opens the database, yet the sales manager sees all of the customers when he or she accesses the database.

When you open a database, the Security button on the status bar gives you a clue about the level of access you have to that database. Click the Security button on the status bar and the Groups and Roles dialog box appears, indicating your access level.

Each person is granted one of seven levels of access to a database:

- **No Access**—This denies you access to the database. You can't read any of the documents in the database, and you can't create new documents.

- **Depositor**—You can create documents but can't read any of the documents in the database—including the ones you create yourself. You might be granted this access level to cast a ballot in a voting database, for example.

- **Reader**—You can read the documents in the database, but you can't create or edit documents. You might have this level of access to a company policy database so that you can read policies but can't create or change them.

- **Author**—As an author, you can create documents but you can't necessarily edit your own documents without additional permission. You can read documents created by others.

- **Editor**—You can do everything an author does, and you can edit documents submitted by you and others. A manager who approves the expense reports submitted by others needs at least editor access to those documents, for example.

- **Designer**—A designer can do everything an editor can, but also can create or change any design elements of the database. To change the design of a form in a database, you must have designer access.

- **Manager**—A manager can access everything a designer can. A manager also can assign and modify the Access Control List (ACL), modify replication settings, and delete a database from the server.

You probably will have at least reader access to the Directory (company Address Book), whereas you have manager access to your Personal Address Book and Mail databases.

Additional permissions in the ACL decide whether you can create documents, delete documents, create personal views and folders, and replicate and copy documents.

ENCRYPTION

When you want to keep your email private, encrypt it. Encrypting scrambles your message so that only the person receiving it can read it.

Each Lotus Notes user has a unique *private* and *public* key that Notes stores as part of the ID file. The public key is also stored in the person document for each user in the Domino Directory. When someone sends you an encrypted mail message, Notes uses your public key from the Domino Directory to encrypt the message. Now, no one but you can read it. At the delivery end, Notes uses your private key from your ID file to decrypt the message so that you can read it.

Encryption can be an important tool for laptop users. If you travel with Notes databases on your laptop, consult your Domino Administrator about how to encrypt databases on your laptop and whether he recommends it.

SIGNATURES

Two "signatures" are available in Notes. One is the signature you attach to your letterhead. The second is an encoded and internal Notes function that prevents a user from masquerading as someone other than herself. To apply a signature to a message, the sender must have a Notes ID and know her password. For example, Jane, a Notes designer, can change her mail memo form to appear with Dorothy's name at the top and in the "from" field. She can send this message out, appearing to be Dorothy. Jane cannot *sign* the message as

Dorothy, however, without knowing Dorothy's password and without having Dorothy's Notes ID. This is why you should protect your password and ID.

When a signature is applied in Notes, you see a message in the status bar that says "Signed by Jane Kirkland." This assures you that Jane created this message (unless, of course, Jane was foolish enough to distribute her password and ID to someone else).

WEB ACCESS TO NOTES MAIL

If you have access to your Notes mail file over the Internet using either WebMail or iNotes Web Access, you can access your mail using a Web browser when you are at a computer on which Lotus Notes is not installed but which has Internet access. Check with your Domino Administrator to see if your organization has these capabilities. If you have this capability, when you access mail from a browser, you will be prompted to enter an Internet username and password.

Your username is the same as the name that displays in the Enter Password dialog box when you log in to Notes (such as Joe Doaks/Philly/Stillwater). You can use just the common name portion of this name, as in *Joe Doaks* or your shortname, *jdoaks*. If you have access to your organization's Domino Directory, open it and then open your Person document. The User Name field lists all the variations of your name you can use, or you can use the Short Name/User ID name. Your Internet password also appears in this document, but all you can see is the code, not the password you need to use.

Your Internet password is usually set and supplied to you by your Domino Administrator, and it *might* be the same as the password you use when you start the Lotus Notes client. However, it is possible that you will need to set your own password. Additionally, you might want to change your Internet password once your Administrator supplies it to you. Check with your Domino Administrator before you change or set your Internet password.

WHEN IS A PASSWORD NOT A PASSWORD?
Your Internet password is not the same as your Notes password, even if both passwords use the same characters. In other words, changing one password does *not* change the other.

You may be prompted to change your password automatically the first time you authenticate with a Domino server over the Web. If not, or if you decide to change the password later, enter the URL for a Web application you access on the server and add **?changepassword** after the name of the database. For example, the URL might be

http://servername.organization.com/database.nsf?changepassword.

The Change Password screen appears, and you must enter your old Internet password first. Then you enter your new password (be careful not to make any typing mistakes), and enter it again to confirm it. Click the **Submit** button.

INDEX

C

G-H

Island location, 187
    working offline, 260
Italic icon, 208
items, To Do
    creating, 157
    private, 157
    setting dates, 158
    setting priorities, 161
    setting reminders, 161
    setting repetitive tasks, 159

J-K-L

keyboard hotkeys, formatting
    paragraphs, 211
keyboard shortcuts
    formatting text, 208
    undoing actions, 204
keyword fields, 205

labels, printing, 177
Language button, 86
launching Notes Minder, 118-119
length of day, calendar setting, 108
less than or equal to sign (<=),
    search operator, 100
less than sign (<), search operator,
    100
letterheads (mail), 65. See also
stationery
    changing, 105
    selecting, 105
Letterhead tab, 105
line spacing, paragraphs, formatting,
    209-210
Link Message command (Special
    menu), 228
Link Messages, 227-229

links, 214
    Anchor, 215, 218
    creating, 214
    Database, 215, 218
    Document, 215-217
    types of, 214
    View, 215, 218
    viewing, 217
list boxes, 13
List by name option (Select Address
    dialog box), 38
List icon, 211
lists
    paragraphs, formatting, 210
    Select Folder to Place Shortcut
        In, 119
    To Do, 10
Load Search button, 200
loading searches, 101
local databases, 80
local replica, 245, 249-250
Location button, 86
location documents, 180, 187
    editing, 187
    Internet, 251
    Island, 187, 251, 260
    Office, 251
    settings for Web browsers, 180
    Travel, 251, 253
locations
    choosing, 6
    folders, specifying, 59
Lock ID command (Tools menu), 21
locking, User IDs, 20-21
Look In option (Select Address
    dialog box), 38
Lotus Applications command
    (Programs menu), 118
Lotus Applications menu commands,
    118

How can we make this index more useful? Email us at indexes@quepublishing.com

O

P